NUMBER 402

THE ENGLISH
EXPERIENCE

ITS RECORD IN EARLY PRINTED BOOKS
PUBLISHED IN FACSIMILE

JOHN NORDEN

SPECVLVM BRITANNIAE
DISCRIPTION OF
MIDDLESEX

n. p. 1593

DA CAPO PRESS
THEATRVM ORBIS TERRARVM LTD.
AMSTERDAM 1971 NEW YORK

The publishers acknowledge their gratitude
to the Curators of the Bodleian Library, Oxford
for their permission to reproduce
the Library's copy (Shelfmark: Wood 467)
and the maps from Shelfmark: Arch.G.e.41(10)

Library of Congress Catalog Card Number:
70-171777

S.T.C. No. 18635
Collation: $A\text{-}G^4, H^2$ + 3 folding plts.

Published in 1971 by

Theatrum Orbis Terrarum Ltd.,

O.Z. Voorburgwal 85, Amsterdam

&

Da Capo Press

- a division of Plenum Publishing Corporation -

227 West 17th Street, New York, 10011

Printed in the Netherlands

ISBN 90 221 0402 8

DIEV ET MON DROIT

SPECVLVM BRITANNIAE.

The first parte

*An historicall, & chorographicall discrip
tion of Middlesex. Wherin are also al-
phabeticallie sett downe, the names of the
cyties, townes, parishes hamletes, howses of
name &c. W th direction spedelie to
finde anie place desired in the
mappe & the distance
betwene place and
place without compasses.*

CVM PRIVILEGIO

By the travaile and vew
of Iohn Norden. Anno 1593

TO THE HIGH,
AND MOST MIGHTY
EMPRES, ELIZABETH, BY THE
DIVINE PROVIDENCE, QVEENE OF
ENGLAND, FRAVNCE, AND
IRELAND, POWERFVL PROTEC-
TOR OF THE FAITH, AND VNDOV-
TED RELIGION OF THE MES-
SIAH, THE MOST COMFORTABLE
NVRSING MOTHER OF THE
ISRAEL OF GOD, IN
THE BRITISH
ISLES.
HER HIGHNES LOYALL SVBIECT
IOHN NORDEN, IN ALL HV-
MILITIE, CONSECRATETH
HIS SPECVLVM
BRITANNIÆ.

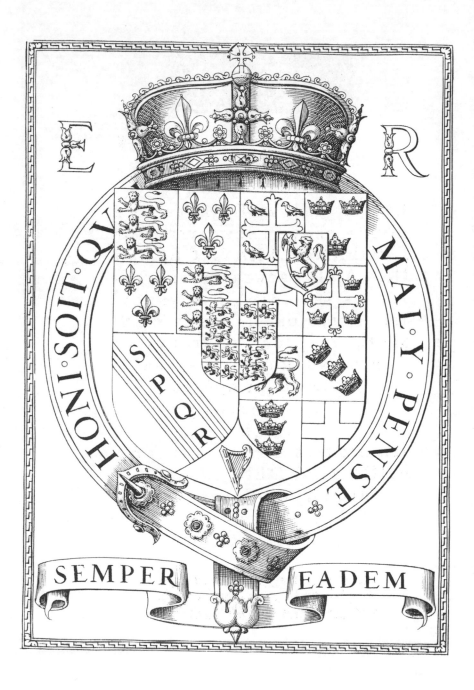

TO THE RIGHT HONORA-
BLE SIR William Cecill
KNIGHT, LORDE Bvrghley,
Lord high Treasurer of England,
and of hir Maiesties most Ho-
norable priuy Counsell.

Auing by your Ho-
norable meane (my
good Lord) obtei-
ned, at the hands of
my sacred S o v e-
reigne, gratious
passe, & priuiledge,
for mine intended
labours, the description of famous England. I cannot but, in dutie, render vnto
your Honor, condigne thanks, and withall
diligence, and dutifull endeuour, proceed
therein : hoping, that although (in regarde
of my long sicknes & other impediments)
this beginning carrie not so absolute perfection, as in your wisedome may be requi-
red : yet may I enioy your patient directi-
ons, and gratious assistance, I shall effect
the residue more fully to answere Honorable expectation.

Your Honors in all dutie,

Io. Norden

TO THE CONSIDERATION
OF THE HONORABLE,
WISE, AND LEARNED.

Lthough I cannot but confeſſe that I am the vnwoorthieſt of manie in this lande, (and eſpeciallie in theſe daies of ſurpaſſing knowledge) to vndertake (after other farre more deſeruing) ſo commendable a labor: which requireth arte, induſtrie, learning, countenance, and charge, wherewith I am not ſo fullie furniſhed as ſome other. Yet it may pleaſe you (in fauour) to accept of my willingnes, and beare with my wants : And the rather for that it hath beene helde heeretofore an excuſe(in curteſie) *Velle bene*, though in this age (more ripe in experience) is expected, *Optimè perficere :* which neither, altogither eſcapeth without emulation : I, as ouercome with a deſire to take pains to profite my Countrey, reſt vndoubtfull, that the wiſe, and learned , will not onely tollerate, but in fauour accept this ſimple beginning.

The fruits of my trauell tend not alone to my ſelfe in priuate, but to the publike eaſe of many. In lieu whereof, my hope and deſire is, that he that can reprooue, will friendly reforme what he findeth iuſtly faultie. So ſhall my proceedings grow to more perfection: and I by all endeuour will ſeeke to accompliſh what may anſwere diſcret affections.

Nihil vbique placet.

IO. NORDEN.

I T is to be noted, that for your eaſe I haue in the liſt of the Map of the Shire, ſet downe certaine deuiſions, letters, and figures : the deuiſions are in ſteed of a ſcale of the miles, the leſſer cõ-taining one, the greater two miles. The letters and figures ſerue for the preſent finding of any place deſired in the Map, which places are found in the Alphabet with the letter and figure that direct to the place deſired. A matter of ſo great facilitie as needeth no example.

He that deſireth to know the diſtance betweene places in the Map without compaſſes, the vſe of the croſſing lines, which ſerue for a vniuerſall ſcale through the Map, anſwe-reth his deſire.

Whereas in the collection of the Alphabeticall table, there are heere and there diſperſed houſes of Nobility & Gentrie. I craue fauorable conſideration, though I haue not ſo narrow-ly acquired their intereſtes, as that may aſſure me, that they be all the true ownoures in fee, of the places which they are reſident in, which thing to obſerue; as it doth not meerely ap-pertaine to my purpoſe, So were it a matter intricate, and the more, for that information (often vncertaine) muſt be of ne-ceſſitie, the chiefeſt guide therein. Such therefore as I con-ceiue moſt doubtfull for want of certaine certificat, I haue noted with two ſtarres thus, * *

Alſo in this commencement of my trauailes, I haue obſer-ued certain funeral monuments with the armes (if any ther-on reſt vndefaced) which if it may be fauorably conceiued, I ſhall with more diligence obſerue the like hereafter, whereby may be preſerued in perpetuall memory, that which time may deface, and ſwallow vp in obliuion. Alſo by this obſeruation, many may be certified of the places where their aunceſtors and allies are interred, and by the coates finde out their vn-knowne kinred.

Negotium ex negotio ſeritur.

IOHN NORDEN.

Io. Nordeni vale, ad primam partem sui SPECVLI BRITANNIAE.

VAde liber *Speculi* caput es, tua mēbra ſequentur,
  ELISABETHA potens, arxq; patrona tua eſt.
Quid ſi in te dominúmq; tuum ruet inuidus audax?
  Tu dominúſque tuus, tutus inermis eris.
Ito foràs, valeáſque liber, te forte ſagaces
  Incultum voluant: cætera culta forent,
Ibis in orbe gerens, quamuis tua fata libelle,
  Ardua principio, ſpes meliora canit.
ELISABETHA valens, altiſſima, maxima, firma,
  Auxilium, quandò, ſceua procella venit.
Hæc tibi conductum, non te pericula tangunt,
  Digna patrona illa eſt, ſpeſque, saluſque tua.

The Saxon Alphabet.

A	b	c	ꝺ	Є	ꝼ	ᵹ	h	i	k	l	M	n	o	p	q	ꞃ	ẟ	ꞅ	ꞇ	u	ƿ	X	x	y
a	*b*	*c*	*d*	*e*	*f*	*g*	*h*	*i*	*k*	*l*	*m*	*n*	*o*	*p*	*q*	*r*	*S*	*s*	*t*	*u*	*w*	*X*	*x*	*y*

ꝼЄ	ꝼꞃ	Ð	ð	þ	⁊	ꝥ
Æ	*æ*	*Th*	*th*	*th*	*and*	*that*

A BRIEFE DECLARATION
OF THE TITLES, INHABITANTS,
DIVISIONS, AND SCITVATION
of *ENGLAND* or *BRITANNIA*
maior: a neceſſary introduction to our
Speculum Britanniæ.

Otwithſtanding it reſteth vncertaine, how, when, and by whom, this our BRITANNIA was firſt peopled, yet to ſatiſfie ſuch as expeɕt the iudgements, and opinions of ſome auncient writers concerning the ſame: I thinke it not impertinent to ſcite the affirmation of * *Beroſus*, who ſaith that *Samothes* called alſo *Meſech*, brother to *Gomer* and *Tuball*, called alſo *Dis*, the ſixt ſonne of *Iaphet*, the ſonne of *Noah*, came into this land about 252. yeres after the floud: who called it *Samothea*, 3593. yeeres paſt: in which name it continued vntill *Albion*, the ſonne of *Neptune*, (who diſcended of *Cham*) entred the ſame, and chaunged the name of *Samothea* into ALBION. This *Albion* raigned about 562. yeeres after the floud: in the yeere of the worlds creation 2219. 3340. yeeres ſince. *Plinie* calleth it ALVION. *Ptolomey* ἀλυιον.

Strabo Munſter, and others, will haue it ALBION *ab albis rupibus*, of the white ſea clifes, which are in the ſouth coaſt of the lande:

Some others will haue it come of the Greeke worde *Olbion*, which ſignifieth *felix* happie, in regarde of their happines belike that firſt atchiued it. So doth *Strabo* call *Albania*, wherein he placeth the people *Caucaſiæ: felicem habitatu regionem*, a happie countrie to dwell in. So is *Gothia* in the countrey language *terra bona*, a good countrey. Some will haue it ALBION of *Albina Diocleſians* daughter, which hath no probabilitie.

It continued in the name of ALBION 608. yeeres, vntill *Brytus* or *Brutus Iulius*, arriuall, who conquered the ſame about the yeere of the worldes creation 2828. 2734. yeeres paſt. This *Brute* changed the name of ALBION into BRYTANE, and the people *Albiones* into *Brisans*; or after ſome BRVTAYNE of the ſame *Bruse*: y, being turned into v.

B   Some

Beroſus in Chaldant.
Annius in Beroſ.
Cæſar. Com.
* *Some ſuſpeɕt that the hiſtorie of Beroſus, was but counterfeit, falſly fathered vpon his name, & therefore helde of no great authoritie.*

Ringman. in deſ Europæ.

Munſt. Coſm.

Olbion.
Cowp. in Diɕt.

Strabo lib. 4.

Caxton.

Brutes arriuall.
Galf. Monum.
Bale Cent. 1.

Britannia.

Some will haue it BRITANNIA of *Brytona* a nymph of Greece: others rather holde that it ſhoulde take that name of a ſepera-

Twinus in Com.

tion, as M. *Twine* in his Commentaries, who ſaith, *Britannia* is ſo called,ſor that it is *Locus diuorſio ſeparatus ab eo cui adhæſerat:* a place ſeuered from another whereunto it was annexed : and the more to fortifie his reaſon,he coniectureth that this *Britannia* (nowe an apparant Iſland) was ſomtime *Peninſula* annexed vnto the maine of Fraunce ; which no doubt is true,but not ſince the generall in-undation,(by probabilitie) whereby infinite chanels were eaten in the earth, with the rage of ſo violent a floud, and conſequently many Iſlands diſperſed as we ſee in the main Ocean, and middle earth ſeas : forſurely if it had beene *Peninſula,* or *Iſtmus* ſince the

Plinie.

floud, *Plinie* who liued neere 1500.yeeres before M. *Twyne* woulde haue as well mentioned ſuch a conjunction, as that part of the ſea which runneth betweene England and Calleys, which he calleth

Mare Geſſoriacũ.

Mare Geſſoriacum, and which *Ptolomey* calleth *Oceanus Britannicus.* But it ſeemeth that M. *Twyne* ſtandeth vpon the opinion of *Anto-nius Volſcus* a Poet,who dreameth of a paſſage fiue miles in bredth

Seruius Honora-tus.

betweene England and Fraunce : from whom alſo *Seruius Honora-tus* ſeemeth to ſay,that BRITANNIA was *Olim iuncta continenti,* our *Brytaine* was ioined to the maine continent : which ſecrets paſſe our apprehenſion.

*S. Th. Eliot.
Humf. Lloyde.*

Sir *Thomas Eliot* will haue *Britannia* to be *Pritania: Humfrey Lloyd* alſo ſeemeth to ſay it ſhould be *Prid-caine* which ſignifieth beauti-full or white of colour, though the *c* be omitted for more eaſier pronunciation, which maketh it *Pridaine.*

Cæſar Com. lib.4.

Againe,ſome will haue it come of *Brith* a britiſh worde, which ſignifieth painted,which cõiecture I take to come of *Cæſars* words, where he ſaith,*Omnes Britanni glaſto ſe inficiunt,* all the Brytons be-ſmere themſelues, and ſtaine their bodies with oade : of which worde *Brith* and *tania* a Greeke worde which ſignifieth *Regnum* a kingdome,it is ſuppoſed to be aptly called *Brihtania,* the countrey or kingdome of the *Brithtons* or depainted people.

*Goropius Be-canus.
M. Camden.*

Goropius Becanus ſeemeth to hold another opinion,that it ſhould be *Bridania,* wherof M.*Camden* maketh conſtruction,that *Bri* in *Bri-dania* ſhould be free,and ſo to make it *Fredania,*or *Free-denmarke.*

The ſeuerall titles of Brytaine.

Thus is our *Britannia* forced to ſuſtaine ſundry titles vnder one truth, as *Brytannia, Tritania, Prid-caine* or *Pridayne, Brihtania, Bru-tania, Bridania,* and ſuch like : according to as manie ſundrie mens conceits. But were not *Brute* ſo generally reiected in theſe our daies, I could verie eaſely be drawne to aſſure me that it might be moſt truely *Brutania* of *Brute* the ſuppoſed conquerour, and that Greeke worde *tania* a kingdome, though *Brute* were no Greeke, yet might he fitly conioyne this worde *tania* vnto his name *Brute,*

Brutania.

and ſo conclude it *Brutania, Bruti regnum,* the kingdome of *Brute,*

                                 u being

u being nowe turned into *i*, as in other wordes, *Pessimus* is nowe
written *Pessimus*, so are manie other Latine words. Manie of late
yeeres reiect the hystorie of *Brute*, among others, an Abbot sometime of S. Albons, *Iohn* of *Wheathamsted*, who wrote about the yere Io. de Wheat-
of Christ, 1443. who saith plainly, that *Totus processus de Bruto illo,* hampst.
est Poeticus, potius quam historicus: The whole matter of that *Brute*
is Poeticall, (fabulous) rather than a true hystorie. This author
liuing of late daies affoordeth reproofe of the most auncient. But
what antiquitie hath left, and wee by tradition haue recei-
ued, *Ipse sciolus*, dare not absolutelie denie, vppon anie mans
bare coniecture.

　It is at this day called E N G L A N D, *Anglorum terra*, the land of England.
Angles, or Englishmen, the Latins call it *Anglia*, and the French
Angle terre.

　The Angli or Englishmen inhabited part of Germanie whom Angili.
(as I take it) *Ptolomey* calleth *Angili*: and placeth them betweene Ptolomey.
the *Casuari*, & the *Chemæ*, neer the riuer *Visurgis*, now *Weser*, in that
countrey which is now *Westphalia*: who (as *Cæsar* saith) *Prædæ ac* Cæs. Com.
belli inferendi causa, ex Belgis transierunt, came out of *Belgia* the lowe
Countries, to seeke releefe, and to war with the Britons: inuading
most especially that part of the lande which borders vppon the
south east, or Germaine sea, as Kent, Sussex, & Essex. The *Angles* Beda.
or Englishmen inhabited Cambridgeshire, Isle of Elie, Norffolke
and Suffolke ; all which was called *Eastanglia*, and the people *East*
Angles, The Saxons which came also with the *Angles* were disper-
sed and seated in other quarters of the lande, as by the deuision,
and Heptarchie it will appeere.

　The Saxons and Angles draue the Britons into Wales, and Ayn.dom.620.
Cornewall, and other places of refuge. And *Egbert* king of the
west Saxons became sole Monarch of the whole land, and called
the same England, of that part of Germany wherof he was, wherin the *Angili* or Angles inhabited.

　Some other will haue it England of *Anglia*, the name of a Anglia.
Queene, sometime of this Countrey. But what, whence, or when
she was they seeme not to report.

　Others will haue it *Anglia*, scytuate as it were in *Angulo* in a
corner, or newke by it selfe. Which opinion is not altogither to
be reiected, for that *Iulius Solinus* saith, that the sea coast of Gal- Iulius Solinus.
lia had beene the ende of the worlde, but that the Isle of Britaine,
(which standeth alone as it were in an angle) for the largenes
thereof, deserueth the name of another worlde, being seperated
from the rest of the earth, as *Virgil* saith, *Penitus toto diuisos orbe Bri-*
tannor. Iosephus in the oration of king *Agrippa* saith, *The Romaines* Iof.lib.2.cap.26.
sought another world, beyond the great Ocean, sending their hoster into Bri- bel.Iud.
tayne. And *AEgispus* saith, *The Romaines by strength gat another*
B 2　　　　　　　　　　world

AEgif.*lib.2.de*
excid. Hier.
Ant.Volſc.

world beyond the Ocean in Britaine far from them. Antonius Volſcus affirmeth,*Peloponeſum* to be *Vltimum orbem,Britanniam verò alterum or-*
bem: So that it may be ſaide it ſtandeth in *Angulo*, yet it ſeemeth
not thereof to be called *Anglia.*

This our famous B R I T A N N I A (of it ſelfe another world) for
the firtilitie and pleaſantnes thereof, hath been ſought for, conquered, and inhabited of many ſundrie nations.

Aborigines.

The firſt as ſome dreame were *Aborigines* ſuch people as the
earth it ſelfe, without humaine propagation brought foorth : who

Ouid *metamor.*

belike followe *Ouid*, who ſaith , *Cætera diuerſis tellus animalia formis,*
*ſponte ſuo peperit,&c.*But to ſay that men ſhould ſpring of the earth
ſince *Adam* diſagreeth from the word of God, whereby we learne
that God created them male and female, to increaſe & multiply,

Aborigines in
Italie.

& to gouerne all other earthly creatures. There were a people in
Italie,ſo called, and they of very great antiquitie : yet not begot-
ten or ſprong of the earth,but becauſe they were *Vagi*,and *Sine la-*
ribus,wanderers vpon the earth without houſe or home, voide of
all ciuilitie; & becauſe they were vnknowne from whom they deſcended,they were accounted *Nullorum filii*,the children of no fathers , as the Romanes who bluſh not to ſay they are *Deorum filii*,

Giants in Engländ.
Britons.
Ann.mundi 2855
*Deut.*1.28.

deſcended of the Gods.Such might be in this land at the Britons
ariuall , which might bee counted *Indigenæ*, *Vagi*, vnciuill, and
therefore called Giants , as were the *Anakimes* mentioned in the
Scripture.

Yuand.
Do. Toloſ.*lib. de*
*genel.*Iapheth.

Romanes.

But to leaue theſe vnknowne people ; *Yuandus* writeth that our
Britannia was inhabited firſt by Babylonians:But it is not to be de-
nied that the Britons, (whereofſoeuer ſo named) were the firſt
that vnder ciuill regiment poſſeſſed this land. After them the Ro-
mans,whom *Iulius Cæſar* firſt conducted hither:& after him *Claudi-*
us the Emperor came into this land with his Romanes about *An-*

Iulius Cæſar.
Claudius *impe-*
ras.
Pictes,Scots.
Beede.
M. Camden.
Scots afflict the
Britons.

no Chriſti 40. After the Romanes came the Pictes and Scots out of
Scythia (as *Beede* reporteth.) But M. *Camden* taketh them to bee
Britons which fled into the north parts for feare of the Romanes.
The Scots poſſeſſing the North parts of Britaine , *Albania* nowe
Scotland,greatly afflicted the Britons,of the South, who craued
aide of the Saxons, and they with the Angles ariuing: in proceſſe
of time ſubdued the Britons, and poſſeſſed the lande, driuing the
Britons into *Cambria* now Wales , into Cornewall and other pla-

Ann.Dom. 1012.
Danes.
William *duke of*
Normandy with
his Normans.

ces of refuge, about the yeere of Chriſt, 430. Then came the
Danes,and diſtreſſed the Saxons neere 200.yeeres.   Laſtlie the
Normans vnder the conduct of *William* duke of Normandie,who
vnder a pretended title ſubiected this lande vnto himſelfe about
the yeere of Chriſt 1066.by which conqueſt he is intituled W I L-
L I A M the C O N Q V E R O R, who inforced all the inhabitants to
ſweare vnto him fealtie , faith, and true allegeaunce, and being
quietlie

quietlie setled in his kingdome, caused this land to be described and exactly surueied about the 15. yeere of his raigne, wherein he caused to be obserued, how many hides of land, there were in his kingdome, the value of euery hide, and who possessed it: which suruey resteth in record at Westminster in a booke called *Doomes day*, or the role of *Winchester*. The vsuall account of lande at this day in Englande is by acres, yardes, carewes, hydes, knightes fees, cantreds, baronies and counties.

Xiphilinus diuideth this land into *Britanniam Superiorem*, & *Inferiorem*: *Ptolomey* into *Magnam* & *Paruam*: *Sextus Rufus*, who liued vnder the Emperor *Valentinian*, hath *Britanniam primam*, & *secundam flauiam*, and *Maximam Cæsariensem*, another part added called *Valentia*, remembred by *Marcellinus*. It was also deuided into *Loegria*, *Cambria*, and *Albania*, called also *Caledonia*, which are nowe England, Wales, and Scotland.

It was deuided into seauen kingdomes by the *Saxons*, after, into Prouinces, Shires or Counties, all which were enhabited by people of seuerall names after *Ptolomey*, as may appeere.

William Conqueror *caused England to be described and surueied. Doomes day book.*

Ex Dione. *England how deuided.*

I. Noþþanhymbþaþic. *regnū* Northumbrorū, the kingdome of the Northumbers.	Northumberland & part of SCOTLAND. Westmerland. Cumberland. The Bish. of Durham or Dunelms. Yorkeshire. Lancashire.	Brigantes
2. Myþcnaþic *regnum Merciorum*, the kingdome of Mercia.	Cheshire. Shropshire. Staffordshire. Warwickeshire. Worcestershire.	Cornaui.
	Nottinghamshire. Lincolneshire. Northamptonshire. Rutlandshire. Leicestershire. Derbishire.	Coritani.
	Glocestershire. Oxfordshire.	Dobuni.
	Buckinghamshire. Bedfordshire. Part of Hartfordshire.	Cattieuchlani.
	Herefordshire, part of the	Silures.

Huntingdonshire

Huntingdonſhire part of the ICENI.

3. peꞃꞇƿeax- naꝑic, *occidu* *orum Saxonum* *regnum*, the kingdome of *Weſt Saxons.*	Berkeſhire. Hamſhire. Wilſhire. Somerſetſhire. Dorſetſhire. Deuonſhire. Cornewall.	Atreba- tii. Belgæ. Durotriges. Dammo- nii.
4. Suꝧeaxna- ꝑic, *Auſtraliũ* *Saxonum reg-* *num* the king- dome of *South* *Saxons.*	Suſſex. Surrey.	Regni.
5. Cenꞇꝑic *reg-* *num Cantiorum* the kingdom of *Kent.*	Kent.	Cantii.
6. Eaꞃꞇanꝫla- ꝑic *regnũ ori-* *entaliũ Anglo-* *rũ*, the kingdõ of *Eaſt Angles.*	Norfolke. Suffolke. Cambridgeſhire. The Ile of *Elie.*	Iceni.
7. Eaꞃꞇƿeax- naꝑic *regnum* *orien. Saxonum* the kingdom of *Eaſt Saxons.*	Eſſex. Middleſex, and part of HERTFORDSHIRE.	Trino- bantes.

**7. king-
domes
of the
S A X-
O N S.**

Buſhoprikes in
England.

These ſeauen kingdomes containe 39 ſhires, which are deuided into 22. Biſhopricks, namely, *Caunterbury, Rocheſter, Londõ, Chicheſter, Wincheſter, Saliſburie, Exceter, Bath & Wels, Worceſter, Gloceſter, Hereforde, Couentrie & Lichfield, Lincolne, Elie, Norwich, Oxford, Peterborrough, & Briſtow*, in number 18. vnder the Archb. of Caunterburie Primate of England. *Yorke, Durham, Cheſter*, and *Carelyle*, 4. vnder the Archbiſhop of Yorke.

CAMBRIA, WALES, in- habited by	Flintſhire. Denbi h. Mongomery. Merioneth. Caernaruan.	Ordoui- ces.

the

Cambria *Wales.* | the Bꞃitꞇea laꞃ or WAL-LIBRI-TANNI, is deuided into 13.ſhires. | Radnor. Brecknocke. Glamorgan. Monmouth. Caermarthen. Penbroke. Gardigan. Angleſey. | Silures. Dimætæ. Mona.

The former Heptarchie, or Countrie of 7. kingdomes, nowe a Monarchie, moſt happely gouerned by the ſole *Empres* thereof moſt renowmed Queene Elizabeth, was deuided into the former prouinces, ſhieres or counties by Alvredvs the fourth ſonne of Adolphvs, & brother to Etheldred, who raigned in the yeere of Chriſt 872. But *Cambria*, now Wales, was diſtinguiſhed by ſhieres, by the famous king Henry the eight: all which ſhieres were deuided into certain parts, which the Saxons called Ꝺꞃihinᵹaꝼ which we cal leꝥꞃ or lathes, theſe deuiſions are yet in Kent: and Yorkeſhire at this day is diuided into Rydings, which may be alſo called Ꝺꞃihinᵹaꝼ, all which parts conteine in them certain hunꝺꞃeꝺꞃ, in euerie of which was conteined ten ꞇeoꝥunᵹeꞃ, of vs called Tithings, conteining ten men, wherof it was called alſo ꞇienmenꞇale, a colledge or corporation of ten men, & the officer of this Tithing the Saxons called ꞇeoꝥunᵹmon, of vs (eſpeciallie in the Weſt) a Tythingman: in ſome places, as in Northamptonſhire, a Therdbarrow: ſo that ten of theſe Tithings yeelded a 100 men, whereof the Engliſh call it at this day a Hundred (though the number of the men be now vncertaine) the Latines call it *Centuria*. In ſteede of Tithings, (eſpecially beyonde Trent,) they haue Wapétaches, which the Saxons called ꝥe ponꞇacꞃ, which tooke that name of the view of weapons, and where the Tenaunts deliuered vp their weapons vnto their Lords. The officers of theſe petite deuiſions or Tythings, are in Kent called Bonꝥeꞃealooꝥꞃ, the chiefeſt or eldeſt pledges as M. *Lamberde* moſt expert in the Saxon toung affirmeth.

The word *Shire* commeth of the Saxon Verbe Ꞩcyꝥan, which ſignifieth to cut or to deuide. Euerie of theſe Shires in time paſt was gouerned *per Comitem*, whom we now call Earle, who was *quaſi præfectus regius*, the kings Lieutenant, who of the Saxons was called Eonle, of whom euery Shire is called a Countie, a *Comite*, of the Earle. But of later time there hath beene, and is yeerely choſen in euery ſhire, an officer by the Prince, which in Latine is called *Vicecomes*, as one appointed *vice Comitis* in the Earles ſteed, we call him the Sherife, the Saxons called him Ꞩcyꞃeᵹeꞃeꝼa, the Reeue of the Shire, for ᵹeꞃeꝼa is an officer to collect rents, and other reuenues, and to execute things vnder, & for another,

the

Manie sortes of Reeues.

the Germaines at this daie haue Burgreeue of the Saxons ƿoɲ-ʒʒeɲeʁa, the Mayor of a Towne, Margreeues, whom we cal Wa-terbaylifes: a Landigreue whom we call the Reeue of a Mannor.

The length of Brytaine and the bredth.

Pliny, Gildas Solinus, and *Martianus* do agree, that this our BRITANNIA MAIOR is 800. miles in length, including also Scotland: and *Martianus* faith, it is in bredth 300. miles: in which dimenfuration they feeme to account after the Italian meafure,

The fuppofed breadth & length of Englande by ftatute meafure.

which is leffe then our myles: yet were England meafured accor-ding to the true and exact menfuration prouided and allowed by ftatute, it woulde appeere to be of greater length & breadth, then thefe authors account. An Italian mile containeth *mille paffus ma-*

A myle A furlong. A pearch.

iores, or *Geometricos* a 1000.paces of fiue foote to the pace, which is also a fadome. And our Englifh mile is eight furlongs, euery fur-long 40.pearches, euery pearch 16.foote, and halfe, which maketh 5280. foote, which is more then the Italian mile by 56. paces. But our ordinary mile exceedeth both the Italiã, & true Englifh mile.

The fertilitie of England.

The forme of this land is Trianguler, much like Cicilia an Ifland in the middle earth fea. The center of this land which I take to be about Titburie caftle, hath latitude about 52.degrees, 50.minuts, and longitude 21.degrees 28 minuts. This our BRITANNIA for the fertility & fruitfulnes therof, matcheth the beft, yeelding fuch generall commodities, & in fuch abundance, that it may be faid:

> *Albion emporiis, tellus opulenta marinis,*
>> *fertilis omnigenum rerum :*   Another faith,
> *Anglia non fegetes effundit diuite vena?*
>> *Pafcua non pingui fertilitate tument?*
> *In gremio fluuiis riui mifcentur amænis,*
>> *Gurgitibus rapidis & vada pura meant.*
> *Nobilis antiquo nutat cum robore quercus.*
>> *Et nemorum grato fpirat odore viror.*
> *Vifceribus mediis errant pretiofa metalla,*
>> *Diuitiæ crefcunt intus, opefque foris.*

It were too long to recite the particuler fruites, and rare com-modities it yeeldeth, all which are knowne to the worlde, as the Cofmographicall Poet faith, *Omnia funt fama totũ vulgata per orbem.*

England moft happie in the vfe of the Gofpell.

And aboue all other bleffings it hath greateft caufe to reioyce in the free vfe of the true knowledge of Chrift, wherein it trium-pheth aboue all other kingdomes or Countries of the world, moft happely therin maintained, (vnder the mightie king of kings, ce-leftiall Iehouah) by the facred hand of the moft imperial Queene ELIZABETH, the fruits of whofe happie raigne who can enioy, & not vnfeinedly commend hir fafetie, and happie continuance, vnto that all fufficient God, who beyond expectation, in fauour, commended hir to vs? in regarde whereof our Englande may be truely called OLBION a happie Countrie.

The first part, conteining a briefe Historicall and Chorographicall discription of MYDDLESEX.

Auing thus briefely touched the generall, I purpose to proceede to the particular descriptions of this our BRITANIA: wherein (imitating the artificial Painter, who beginneth alwaies at the head, the principall part of the bodie:) I thought it not vnfit to begin my *Speculum Britaniæ* with MYDDLESEX, which aboue all other Shyres is graced, with that chiefe and head Citie LONDON: which as an adamant draweth vnto it all the other parts of the land, and aboue the rest is most vsuallie ferquented with hir Maiesties most regall presence.

The causes why Myddlesex is the first part of Speculum Britaniæ.

Of MIDDLESEX, and of the Trinobantes.

T is called MIDDLESEX of the *middle Saxons*, for that they inhabited that part betweene the *East Saxons*, *West Saxons*, and *South Saxons*.

Myddlesex why so called.

MIDDLESEX was a percel of that countrey wherin (as *Cæsar* saith) dwelled the *Trinobantes* whom *Ptolomy* calleth *Trinoantes*, omitting the b. some call them *Trinouantes*, putting u. for b.

Myddlesex parte of the Trinobantes.
Cæsar Com.
Ptolomey.
Galfr.Moun.

The chiefe Citie of these *Trinobantes*, was then called *Trinobantum*, of some held to be *Colchester* of some *London*; *Beede* saith that *London* was the chiefe Citie of the *East Saxons*, If so, then of necessitie, of the *Middle saxons*, and consequently of the *Trinobantes*; yet *Tacitus* saith, that *London* was not *Trinobantum*; nor the people *Trinobantes*, neere *London*, and his reason is that if the *Trinobantes* had beene neere *London*, they would not haue suffered *Suetonius* to haue passed thither; which argument *Humfrey Lloyde* seemeth to confute in this manner. The *Trinobantes* (saith he) being *Suetonius* enemies, would haue as well preuented him in the inner part of the countrey, as neere *London*, considering that *Suetonius* came from the Isle of *Anglesey*, marching through the whole countrey. So that in what place soeuer the *Trinobantes* were resident, they could not be ignorant of his passage.

Colchester.
London the Citie of the East Saxons and Trinobantes.
Corn.Tacitus.

Humf.LLoyd.

Polydore Virgile, a man of no great credite, as touching his hi-storie, affirmeth from some other that *Trinobantum* was *Northamp-ton*, and the *Northamptonshire* men *Trinobantes*, and his reason is for that the countrey men in their language called that place *Tran-ton*, which hath no such semblable consonance with *Trinobantum* that he, or any other, should seeke *Trinobantum* in that part of *Bri-taine*.

Master *Camden*, a singuler scrutator of antiquities seemeth to hold (but not absolutely) that the *Trinobantes* should be so called, of the brytish word *Trenant*, which signifieth townes scytuate in the valley. But *Cæsar* saith, they inhabited *Prope firmissimam ea-rum regionum ciuitatem*, neere the most strongest Citie in those countries; which as I take was *London*.

The lymites and principall bounds
of MYDDLESEX.

MYDDELSEX is scituate in the south east parte of this lande, bordering vpon the north, vpon *Hertfordshire*. On the east vpon *Essex*, deuided thence by the riuer *Lea*, and the *Meere ditch* : on the south vpon *Surrey*, hauing the most famous riuer *Thamise*, the bound and lymite betweene them, and on the West vpon *Buckinghamshire*, *Colne* riuer and the *Shire ditch*, being the deuision betweene them.

That famous riuer which is commonly of vs called *Temes*, is of *Ptolemey* called *Iamesa æstuarium*, of *Plinie Iamesais*; of *Cæsar Tamesis*. It seemeth to be compact of two names of riuers, *Tame* and *Ise*, which two riuers meete neere *Wallingford* in *Barkeshire*, where after a familier manner, they louingly conioyne and vnite them selues, and after a kinde of Matrimoniall order, of two they become one *Tame*, and *Ise*, becommeth *Thamise* holding that name, growing more and more famous, vntill with great pride it saluteth the maine sea. The like coniunction of names is in *Palestina* or the *holy land*, where that famous riuer *Iardan*, is compact of *Iar*, which riseth neere *Mara*, towardes *Damascus*, and *Dan* which riseth neere, and taketh name of the Citie of *Dan*, both rising out of the mountaines *Lybanon*, and meete at *Cæsaria Philippi*, where, these two *Iar*, and *Dan*, become *Iardan*, as the Poet saith. *Iordannisque sacer geminis è fontibus ortus*.

The riuer of *Thamise* ebbeth and floweth as farre as *Richmond*, sometime farther, some time not so farre, neere sixtie miles from the maine sea.

It hath beene obserued and affirmed by some that this riuer doth not easely increase with land waters. *Sit experientia Iudex*.

The

The riuer *Lea*, of the *Saxons* liʒa is a proper riuer, heretofore, (as some affirme) nauigable, and that shipping passed through the same, from the *Thamise* to *Hartford*. Barges haue of late passed that way, to *Ware*, which was granted by Acte of Parliament about the eighteent yeer of the raigne of Queene ELIZABETH, but for some causes of late discontinued. This riuer for the most part deuideth MIDDLESEX and *Eastsex*. But there is a ditch called the *Meere ditch*, about two miles and a halfe in length, betweene *Waltham* abbey, and *Higham* hill bridge which is cut into the mershes and passeth through the same, for a distinction of the boundes betweene the two shires.

Meere ditch.

Colne riuer is the deuision betwcen MIDDLESEX and *Buckingham* shire, But that a ditch called the *Shire ditch*, which seemeth to haue been forced into MIDDLESEX, about two miles in length, north of *Colnebroke*.

Colne riuer.
Shire ditch.

Through this riuer as some affirme, haue passed shipping to Saint *Albans*. *Minime credendum*.

The nature of the soyle and fertilitie of MYDDLESEX.

MYDDLESEX is a small Shire, in length not twentie myles, in circuite (as it were by the ring) not about 70. myles, yet for the fertilitie thereof, it may compare with any other shire: for the soyle is excellent, fat and fertile and full of profite: it yeeldeth corne and graine, not onelie in aboundance, but most excellent good wheate, especiallie about *Heston*, which place may be called *Granarium tritici regalis*, for the singularitie of the corne. The vaine of this especiall corne seemeth to extend from *Heston* to *Harrow* on the hill, betweene which as in the mid way, is *Periuale*, more truely *Pureuale*. In which vale is also *Northold*, *Southold*, *Norcote*, *Gerneford*, *Hayes*, &c. And it seemeth to extend to *Pynner*, though with some alteratiō of the soile. It may be noted also how nature hath exalted *Harrow* on the hill, which seemeth to make ostentation of it scituation in the *Pureuale*, from whence, towardes the time of Haruest, a man may beholde the fields round about, so sweetely to addresse themselues, to the siecle, and sith, with such comfortable aboundaunce, of all kinde of graine, that the husbandman which waiteth for the fruits of his labours, cannot but clap his hands, for ioy, to see this vale, so to laugh and sing.

The length and circuit of Middlesex.

Middlesex fertile.

Heston.

Piriuale or pureuale.

Harrow on the hill.

Yet doth not this so fruitefull soyle yeeld comfort, to the wayfairing man in the wintertime, by reason of the claiesh nature of soyle: which after it hath tasted the Autume showers, waxeth both dyrtie and deepe : But vnto the countrie swaine it is as a sweete and pleasant garden, in regard of his hope of future profite, for

The deepe, and dirtie loathsome soyle,
Yeelds golden gaine, to painefull toyle.

The industrious and painefull husbandman will refuse a pallace, to droyle in these golden puddles.

Tandeane.

This part of MYDDDLESEX may for fertilitie compare with *Tandeane,* in the west part of *Somersetshire.* But that *Tandeane,* farre surpasseth it for sundrie fruites, and commodities, which this countrie might also yeelde, were it to the like imployed: but it seemeth they onely couet to maintaine their auncient course of life, and obserue the husbandrie of their fathers, without adding, any thing to their greater profite.

Middlesex bewtified with faire buildinges.

This shire is plentifullie stored, and as it seemeth beautified, with manie faire, and comely buildinges, especially of the Merchants of *London,* who haue planted their houses of recreation not in the meanest places: which also they haue cunningly contriued, curiously beautified, with diuers deuises, neatly decked with rare invencions, inuironed with Orchards of sundrie delicate fruites, gardens with delectable walks, arbers, allees, and great varietie of pleasing dainties : all which seeme to be beautifull ornaments vnto this countrie. But who so turneth his eies vnto the stately & most princely pallaces of Queene ELIZABETH in many parts of this shire most sweetely scituate, garnished with most princelie delights, beholding also the houses of Nobilitie , may laie as *Vadian* of a fruitefull and pleasant place in *Egypt, Facies istius terre*

Vad Cosm.

pulcherima est, &c. The face or superficies of this countrey, is most beautifull, the fields fresh and greene, the valleyes delightfull to behold, the townes villages and stately buildings enterlaced with the pleasant woodes are glorious to be scene.

Of the Ecclesiasticall and Ciuill
gouernment of this Shire.

FOr matter concerning Church gouernment, and order, this shire is vnder the iurisdiction of the bishop of London; which See sometime did belong to the Archbishop, vntill S. *Augustines* time, who was called the Apostle of *Englande,* he turned the Archbishops See from *London* to *Caunterburie,* where it continueth.

And whereas all other shires within this land, for the most part, haue a perticular officer yeerely elected by hir Maiestie,

Sherife of Middlesex.

called a *Sheryfe Shere-Reeue,* or *Reeue* of the shire : this shire by charter made by King IOHN, *Quinto Iulii anno regni sui* 1. is in

that

that point, vnder the high officer of the Citie of *London* the MA-
IOR : who by force of the fame charter, yeerely conftituteth a
Sherife, within the fame: who alfo is accountable vnto the faide
Citie for all matters appertaining to his faid office.

Euerie Alderman that hath beene Maior of *London* is Iuftice of
peace in MYDDLESEX.

Hundreds within MYDDLESEX
diftinguifhed with thefe letters
in the MAPPE.

A	*Edmondton* or *Edelmeton.*	*Hundreds.*
B	*Goare.*	
C	*Ofelfton.*	
D	*Iftlewoorth.*	
E	*Elthorne.*	
F	*Spelthorne.*	

Market Townes in MYDDLESEX.

Weftminfter.　　　　　　　　　　　　　　　*Market towes.*
Brentforde.
Stanes,
Vxbridge,
　　Harrow on the hill, was a market towne in the time of
　　Doct. *Bordes* perigrination as appeereth by a little Trea-
　　tife of his in writing.

It is to be noted that this fhire hath in it manie Chappels of
eafe, that haue the name of parifh Churches : as *Vxbridge* a market towne belongeth to great *Hellingdon* : *Brentford* a market town
belongeth to great *Eling,* manie mo there are within this fhire
which to expreffe would be too tedious.

Houfes of Lawe.

THere are two houfes of *Iudges* and *Searieants,* called *Serieantes
Innes,* the one in Fleeftreere the other in Chauncerie Lane.

　　Innes of Courte are fower.
Inner Temple.
Middle Temple.
Lyncolnes Inne.
Greyes Inne.

　　　　　　　　　　　　　　　　　　　　　　　Innes

Innes of the Chauncery 8.

Clyffords Inne.
Dauydes or *Thauyes Inne.*
Furniuals Inne.
Barnards Inne.
Staple Inne.
Clements Inne.
Newe Inne.
Lyons Inne.

Battles in MYDLESEX noted thus ✱

Polid. vir.
Tho. Walſ.

NEere *Barnet* in *Enfielde Chace*, was a battle fought between EDWARD the fourth, and the fauourites of HENRIE the sixt.

Tho. Walſ.

    Neere *Brentforde* was a conflict betweene *Edmond Iron-side* and the Danes.

Parkes of hir Maiesties within
MYDDLESEX.

THis Shire is plentifully furnished with hir MAIESTIES *Parkes*, for princely delights, exceeding all the kingdome of *Fraunce*, wherein are not so manie, (if the discourse be true which is made of a debate betweene an Heraulde of *England*, and a Herauld of *Fraunce*) where it is affirmed that there are in all that Region but two *Parkes*: In MYDDLESEX are ten of hir MAIESTIES.

S. Iames Parke.
Hyde Parke.
Marybone Parke.
Hanwoorth Parke.
Kenton Parke.
Hampton Courte Parkes, two.
Enfielde Parkes, two.
Twickenham Parke, disperked.

Hilles of name.

Harrow hill.
Hamſted hill.
Highgate hill.

Olde

Olde and auncient highwaies
now vnaccuftomed.

THe old and auncient high waie to high *Bernet*, from *Porte-* Poole, now *Grayes Inne*, as alfo from *Clerkenwell*, was through a lane, on the eaft of *Pancras Church*, called *Longwich lane*, frō thence, leauing *Highgate* on the weft, it paffed through *Tallingdone lane* and fo to *Crouch ende*, and thence through a Parke called *Harnfey great parke*, to *Mufwell hill*, to *Coanie hatch*, *Fryarne Barnet*, and fo to *Whetftone*, which is now the common high way to high *Bernet*. This auncient high way, was refufed of wayfaring men, and carriers, by reafon of the deepenes and dirtie paffage in the winter feafon: In regard whereof it was agreed betweene the Bifhop of *London*, and the Countrie, that a newe waie fhoulde bee layde forth through the faid Bifhops parks, beginning at *Highgate hill*, to leade (as nowe is accuftomed) directly to *Whetftone* : for which newe waie all cartes, carriers, packmen, and fuch like tra-uellers, yeelde a certaine tole vnto the Bifhop of *London*, which is fermed (as is faid at this daie) at 40. *li. per annum*. and for that pur-pofe, was the gate erected on the hill, that through the fame all trauellers fhoulde paffe, and be the more aptlie ftaide for the fame tole.

Another auncient high waie which did leade to *Edgworth*, and fo to *Saint Albons*, was ouer *Hampfted* heath, and thence to, and through an old lane, called *Hendon wante*, neere *Hendon*, through which it paffed to *Edgwoorth*, whence it paffed ouer *Brokeley hilles*, through part of *Hertfordfhire*, by *Radnet*, *Colneftreete*, *Saint Stephens*, and *Saint Mychaels*, leauing *Saint Albons*, halfe a mile in the eaft. This way of fome is helde to be *Watlingftreete*, one of the fower high waies, which *Bellinus* caufed to be made, & leadeth (as fome affirme) through *Watling ftreete* in *London*.

Port Poole.

Tallingdon lane.

Highgate tole.

Hendon want.

An Alphabet of the Cities, Townes, Ham-
lets, Villages, and howfes of name within M I D-
DELSEX, conteined in the Map of the Shire, with neceffarie annotations vpon fundrie of them.
The vfe of which Alphabet is fet down,
before to the Reader.

❋

A.

Afcot. E. 8.
Auguftines lodge. H. 18. a lodge in Enfield chace.

Acton

Aɛɛon eaſt F. 14.

Baron of Burford buried. *Aɛɛon* weſt G. 14. The *Barron* of *Burford* died there, as he paſ-ſed from *London,* and is couered with a Marble ſtone, in the yeere of Chriſt 1527.

Aſhford I. 8. So called of the brooke or ford through which men paſſe at that place.

Aſtleham I. 8.

B.

Breakeſpeare. E. 4. The houſe of *George Aſhby* Eſquire.

* *Brockenborrowes* E. 6. There dwelleth *Gomerſale* Gentleman.

Brownſwell E. 4. a Well in the high way from *Highgate* to *Ber-net,* the water whereof is a ſweete refreſhment often times to we-ried and thirſtie poore trauellers, of late reedified by ſome well diſpoſed.

Ewrye ſtreete B. 20. a Hamlet of Enfield.

Buls lodge A. 18. a lodge of Enfield chace.

Belſiſe E. 16. the houſe of *William Wade* Eſquire, one of the clerkes of hir Maieſties preuy Counſell.

Brent riuer. *Brentſtreete* E. 14. So called of the riuer or brooke called *Brent* through which it runneth.

It is to be noted that at this *Brentſtreete* many yeers ſince dwel-led the *Brents,* among whõ was one *Iohn Brent* who died *Anno Chri-ſti* 1467. whoſe aunceſtors before him had there, their reſidence.

This *Iohn* lieth buried at *Hendon* vnder a marble ſtone, with his picture and the time of his diſceaſe: whereby it ſeemeth that the ſtreete tooke name of the *Brentes,* and the brooke of the ſtreete, and heereof alſo doth,

Brentforde H. 12. commonly called new *Brentford* or *Brayne-forde,* or *Market Brentforde* take name, for that *Brent* brooke paſſeth through the towne. This *Brentford* is a market towne, yet no pariſh, but belongeth vnto great *Elinge.* It is called new *Brent-* *Brentford why ſo called.* *ford* as I take it of the late purchaſe of the market which was in the time of king *Edward* the ſixt: for the chappel argueth it of grea-ter antiquity then the other, which hath the name of old *Brentford.* of the river *Brent,* which runneth on the weſt part of the towne, and betweene it and *Syon* entreth into the *Thames.*

Brent, the word how the people take the ſigniſi-cation. This worde *Brent* among the countrey people, of thoſe partes, ſignifieth, and is taken for all brookes, riuers, and currants of wa-ter, therefore is euerie ſmall brooke called the *Brent* among them.

Edm. Ironſides *conflict with the Danes.* Neere vnto this place *Edmond Ironſide,* aſſaulted the *Danes* which he had driuen from the ſiedge of *London,* and there put manie of them to the ſword, and put the reſidue to flight, about *anno Chriſti* 1016. the place appeereth by this carracter ✳.

Brentford

Brentford old H. 14. a little thorowfare.

*Buſhoppes hall F. 22. the houſe of the Lord *Wentwoorth.*

Blackwall, G. 22. neere which is a harbor in the *Thamis* for ſhip- *Blackwall why*
ping, the place taketh name of the blackenes or darkenes of the *ſo called.*
water bankes, or wall at that place.

Brompton G. 16.

* * Boſton G. 12. where dwelleth *Iherome Halley* Eſquire.

Bedfont weſt H. 6.

Bedfont eaſt H. 8.

* Brumſielde C. 20. the houſe of　　*Skevington* Eſquire.

C.

Cannons D. 10.

Crowch ende D. 18.

*Coanie Hatch D. 18. there dwelleth　　*Trot* Gentleman.

Clapton E. 22.

* * Canburie or *Cannonburie* E. 20. a houſe in the hands of
Atee Gentleman. It was builded by prior *Bolton* prior of Saint
Bartholmewes in *Smithfield* in the time of H. 8.

Childes hill E. 16.

Chalcot or *Chalkhill* E. 16.

Cowley F. 6.

Chelſey G. 18. So called of the nature of the place whoſe ſtrond *Chelſey why ſo*
is like the cheſel which the ſea caſteth vp of ſand & pebble ſtones. *called.*
Therof called *Cheſelſey* breefely *Chelſey,* as is *Chelſey* in *Suſſex,* north
of *Chycheſter,* which ſtandeth vpon the very edge of the ſea, as this
*Chelſey on the *Thamiſe.* Queene E L I Z A B E T H hath there a faire
houſe : The Lord *Dacres* hath there a faire houſe.

Cheſwicke H. 14. belonging to a prebend of P aules now in the
handes of Doctor *Goodman* Deane of *Weſtminſter,* where he hath
a faire houſe, whereunto (in the time of any common plague or
ſicknes) as alſo to take the aire, he withdraweth the ſchollers of
the colledge of *Weſtminſter.*

*Colham, Collumbe, or *Colneham,* G. 6. a houſe of the Earle of *Dar-
bies,* which taketh name *Colneham* of the ſcytuation thereof ſo
neere a branch of *Colne* ſtreame.

Colbrooke or *Colnebroke* G. 6. one little part wherof is in M I D-
D L E S E X as farre as the bridge, the reſt is *Buckingham ſhire.*

Craneford H 8. It is ſo called of the forde or brooke called by
the name of *Crane.*

Carleton or *Charleton* K. 8.

D.

Dalis D. 14.

Dryvers hill D. 14.

* Durance B. 20. the houſe of *Robert Wroth* Eſquire.

D　　　　** Durcams*

** *Durhams* B. 14. a houſe in the hands of   *Large* Gentleman.

    Daleſon hill E. 14.

    Dormans well F. 10. the houſe of the *Lo.Dacres.*

    * *Drayton* G. 6. a houſe late the Lord *Pagets.*

E.

Edgeworth D. 12. conſiſting of one maine ſtreete, the weſt ſide whereof belongeth to little *Stanmer* called alſo *Whitchurch* the

poŋþ.   other part hath a church in it ſelfe. poŋþ in the *Saxon* toong ſignifieth a place fruitefull, and fit in regarde of the apt ſcytuation thereof to be inhabited this poŋþ ſtanding on the very edge of the ſhire may be called *Edgeworth*, of ſome but corruptly *Edgeware.*

    Eaſt end D. 16. a member of *Finchley.*

    Edmondſon or *Edelmeton* C. 20. In the Church whereof, are ſundry ancient monuments, the moſt of them defaced, among which is a tombe of gray Marble circumſcribed thus.

Thomas Careleton buried.   *Hic iacent corpora Thomæ Carleton cuiuſdã dni. iſtius villæ qui obiit 21. die Februar: Anno Do- 1447. & Elizabethæ vxo ris eius. filiæ Adæ Francis militis per quam habuit dominium*, whoſe arms are theſe.

Iohn Kirketon buried.   There is alſo one *Iohn Kirketon* Eſquire, whoſe monument is of white free ſtone erected in the ſouth wall of the Church, and ſeemeth as auncient as the Church it ſelfe, but there is no record of the time of his deceaſe, his armes are theſe.

Peter Fabell buried.   There is a fable of one *Peter Fabell* that lyeth in the ſame Church alſo, who is ſaide to haue beguiled the Deuell by pollicie for money, But the Deuell is deceite it ſelfe, and hardly decciued.

                                       There

There lyeth one whoſe name I cannot truly learne, his toumbe is verie auncient, couered with a faire Marble ſtone, his body figured in braſſe, armed with a gorget of Mayle, vnder his feete a Lyon cowchaunt, at his helme, there ſeemeth to be figured a Lyon with his two fore pawes raiſed towardes his mouth, his hinder partes as it were mantuled, it is defaced and much obſcured, his wife is there alſo intombed, on the monument are theſe armes

Edmonton ſtreete C. 20.

Enfield B. 20. ſometime parcell of the land of the Duke of *Lancaſter* now Queene *Elizabeths.* The chace called *Enfield chace* taketh name of this place.

It is called of ſome *Enfen* and ſo recorded, in regarde of the *Enfen.* Fenny ſcytuation of ſome part thereof vpon the marſhes or meeriſh ground, which (though now brought to be good meadow and profitable paſture) it hath beene in time paſt fenney: thereof taking the name *Enfen* or *Infen,* now *Enfielde.* But theſe fenney grounds are now on the eaſt, as the chace in the weſt, profitable neighbors not onely vnto *Enfield,* but to many other poore inhabitants neere.

Elinge called great *Elinge* G. 12. In the Church whereof lyeth buried *Thomas Frowike* ſometime owner of *Gunnersbury* or *Gunwelſbury* an auncient ſeat within the ſame pariſh.

Thomas frowike buried.

Enewey H. 6. a ferme houſe belonging vnto the Deane and chapter of *Weſtminſter.*

Enfielde houſe A. 20. Queene ELIZABETHS, builded by an Earle of *Worceſter.*

F.

Frith called alſo *New hall* D. 14. ſometime the *Therlebyes* now *Richard Weekes* Gentleman, by purchace.

Lord Frowike.

Finchley D. 16. In the Church whereof lyeth the Lord *Frowyke*, Lord chiefe Iuſtice of England, in the time of H. 6. vnder a Marble toombe where hath beene his picture and armes in braſſe, with circumſcription about the toombe, but now defaced, his armes onely remayning in the chauncell window in this manner.

There is alſo another Marble ſtone hauing the picture of a woman whereon is inſcribed thus.

Ioan la feme Thomas de Frowicke giſt icy, & le diſ Thomas Penſe de giſer aueque luy.

Thomas Aldenham.

There lyeth alſo buried vnder a Marble ſtone in the Chauncell of the Church one *Thomas Aldenham* Eſquire ſometime Chirurgion to King *Henrie* the ſixt who died in *Anno* **1431.** his armes.

Fryarne Barnet **C. 18.**

** *Fryarne Mannor* C. 18. Sir *Iohn Popham* knight Lord chiefe Iuſtice of England, ſometime maketh there his abode.

** The *Folde* B. 16. the houſe of

Fulham H. 16. of the *Saxons* called ɼullonham (which as Maſter *Camden* taketh it) ſigniſieth *Volucrum domus*, the habitacle of birdes or the place of fowles, ɼullon and ɼuȝlaɼ in the *Saxon* toong doe ſigniſie fowles, and ƕam or ƕame as much as home in our toong. So that ɼullonƕam or ɼuȝlaɼƕame is as much to ſ..ie, as the home houſe or habitacle of fowle. It may be alſo taken for *Volucrum amnis* the riuer of fowle, for ƕam alſo in many places ſigniſieth *Amnis* a riuer. But it is moſt probable it ſhould be of lande fowle which vſually haunt groues, and cluſters of trees, whereof in this place it ſee-meth hath beene plentie.

* There is an auncient houſe belonging to the ſea of *London* moated aboute. *Henry* the third often lay at this place.

The hoſte of the pagan *Danes* in the time of K. *Alphred* did win

ter

ter there, in the yeere of Chriſt 879. the woodes, and apt ſcytua- *Galfr. mon. Greg.*
tion of the place, for paſſage by water (no doubt) moued them *in paſt.*
thereunto.

Felſham I.8.

Felſham hill I.8.

G.

Gernford F.10. a very fertile place of corne ſtanding in the *pure vale.*

Gunnersbury or *Gunwelsbury* G.14. an auncient houſe well ſcytuate for wood, water, and ayre ſometime the *Frowickes* now belonging to the **Corbets,

S. Gyles in the fielde F.18. erected by *Matylde* Queene to H.1. *Rex. E.3.* for leprous people about *Anno* 1117.

H.

* *Harefield* E.4. There Sir *Edmond Anderſon* knight, Lord chiefe Iuſtice of the common plees, hath a faire houſe ſtanding on the edge of the hill. The riuer *Colne* paſſing neere the ſame through the pleaſant meddowes and ſweete paſtures yeelding both delight, and profit.

Highwood hill D.12. a member of little *Stanmer.*

Hendon D.14. of the *Saxous* ꜧiꝫhenꝺune, which ſignifieth *Hendon why ſo*
Highwood of the plentie of wood there growing on the hils. *called.*

* *Hendon houſe* D.14. the mannor houſe of *Hendon*, Sir *Edward Herbertes* knight : where nowe is often reſident, *Iohn Forteſcue* Eſquier, one of hir Maieſties moſt honorable priuie Counſell, when he taketh the ayre in the Countrey.

Hollicke, D.18. there are noted the foundations of ancient buildings, affirmed by ſome aged men that it hath beene a Towne. but oftentimes, *Immenſa cani ſpirant mendatia folles.*

Harnſey, of ſome *Horneſey*, D.20. a pariſh ſtanding neere the Biſhop of Londons woodes or parkes, which of that place heeretofore had and yet retaine the names of *Harnſey* parkes.

The Church of *Harnſey* is ſuppoſed to be built with the ſtones that came from the ruines of *Lodghill.*

Hadley, B.16.

Holway the lower, E.20.

Holway the vpper, E.18.

Highgate, E.18. a hill ouer which is a paſſage, and at the top of *Highgate why ſo*
the ſame hill is a gate through which all maner paſſengers haue *called.*
their waie; the place taketh the name of the highgate on the hill, which gate was erected at the alteration of the way, which (as is ſaide before) was on the eaſt of *Highgate.*

When the way was turned ouer the ſaide hill to leade through
the

the parke of the Bishop of London as nowe it doth, there was in regard thereof, a tole raised vpon such as passed that way with carriage. And for that no passenger shoulde escape, without paieng tole by reason of the widenes of the waie, this gate was raised, through which of necessitie all traueilers passe. This tole is nowe fermed of the said Bishop at fortie pound *per annum.*

At this place is a free schole builded of bricke by sir ROGER CHOLMELEY knight, sometime Lorde chiefe Iustice of *England* about the yeere of Christ 1564. The pencion of the master is vncertaine : there is no vsher, and the schole is in the disposition of sixe governors or feffees.

Where now the schole standeth, was an Hermytage, and the Hermyte caused to be made the causway betweene *Highgate* and *Islyngton*, and the grauell was had from the top of *Highgate* hill, where now is a standing ponde of water.

There is adioining vnto the schole a chapple for the ease of that part of the countrey, for that they are within the parish of *Pancras* which is distant thence neere two miles.

Vpon this hill is most pleasant dwelling, yet not so pleasant as healthfull, for the expert inhabitants there, report that diuers that haue beene long visited with sicknes, not cureable by Physicke, haue in short time, repayred their health by that sweete salutarie aire.

** At this place   CORNEWALLEYES esquire, hath a verie faire house from which he may with great delight beholde the stately Citie of *London*, *Westminster*, *Greenewich*, the famous river of *Thamyse*, and the countrey towardes the south verie farre.

Hamsted, E. 16. standeth vnder a hill, in a verie healthfull ayre, hauing *London* in verie pleasant perspect. In the church thereof lieth M. ARMIGELL WAADE esquire, in a faire monument of Alablaster raised in the wall of the Chauncell with this inscription.

Memoriæ sacrum.

Optimis & charissimis parentibus ARMI-
GELLO WAADO *è Brigantium antiqua fami-*
lia oriundo, HEN. 8. *&* EDW. 6. *Regum Secretori*
concilio ab epistolis, & in agro Middlesexiano
Eirenarchæ qui in maximarum artium disciplinis,
prudentiaque ciuili instructissimus, plurimarum
linguarum callentissimus, legationibus honoratissi-
mis perfunctus, & inter Britannos Indiarum A-
mericarum explorator primus. Ex duabus coniu-
gibus, ALICIA PATENIA, *&* ANNA MERBVRIA, 20. *liberos*
progenuit, tandemque post vitam, honorifice & pientissimè defunctam an-

*no virginei partus 1568. Mensis Iunii die 20. in domino placide obdormuit.
Et* ALICIAE PATENIAE *quæ patri 17. libros peperit, è quibus duo
mares & tres femellæ, adhuc in viuis exiftunt quæ vita caftiffime & tem-
peratiffimè tranfacta, anno falutis humanæ 1568. animam pientiffimam
Redemptori reddidit.*

GVLIELMVS WAADVS *filius maximus natu, & heres,
Idemque diuæ* ELIZABETHE *Reginæ concilio Secretori ab
epiftolis, hoc monumentum pofuit.*

Harrow on the hill, E. 10. ftanding verie high, in a place both
pleafaunt and fruitefull, and though loftely mounted on a hill,
yet in reafonable fort watered.

In the ile of the church lieth buried M. WILLIAM GERARD
Efquire & DORATHEY his wife, who dwel-
led at *Flamberds,* fo called of the *Flamberdes,*
who fomtime poffeffed the fame, this WIL-
LIAM GERARD deceafed the 15. *Apr.*
1583. and they both lie in a tombe of white
marble, raifed in the wall.

Diuers of the *Flamberds* of *Flamberdes* a
hamlet in *Harrow,* are interred in the fame
Church, among whom is one IOHN FLAM-
ERDS, onwhofe tombe is thus infcribed.

*Ion me do marmore numinis ordine flam tumulatur.
Barde quoque verbere ftigu è funere hic tueatur.*

There is a fchoole in *Harow,* as yet not a free fchoole, but inten-
ted to be, and one IOHN LYONS Gent. hath giuen (after his de-
ceafe to be imployed towards the erection and founding therof,)
300.pound, and 30.pound *per ann.* for a Mafter, and 10.pound for
an Vfher (as it is informed) a prefident good to be followed of the
able.

Hellingdon great F. 6.

In the church lieth buried vnder a tombe couered with a mar-
bell ftone, the Lord STRANGE whofe tombe is circufcribedthus,
Sub hac tumba iacet nobilis IOHANNES *dominus le* STRANGE,
Dominus de Knocking, Mahun, Waffet, Warnell, *&* Lacy, *&*
Dominus de Colham, *vna cum pictura* IAGNETTAE *quondam
vxoris fuæ: quæ quidem* IAGNETTA, *fuit foror* ELIZABETHAE
Reginæ Angliæ *quondam vxoris Regis* EDW.4. *qui quidem* IOHAN-
NES *obiit.15 die Octobris Anno regni Regis* EDW. 4. 17. *quam qui-
dem tumbam* IOHANNA *Domina le* STRANGE *filia & heres
predicti* IOHANNIS *&* IAGNETTAE, *vna cũ pictura* IOHAN-
NAE *ex fumptibus fuis propriis, fieri fecit 1509.*

* *Hayes,* F.8. belongeth to the Lord *Dacres,* and Lord *North.*

Harleftone greene, F. 14.

Hockefdone, F. 20. belonging to a Prebend of Paules.

Hackeney

William Ger-
rard efquire bu-
ried.

Flamberds.

Iohn Lyons *bis
gift to the erection
of a free fchoole.*

Lorde Strange
buried.

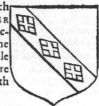

Chriſtopher Vrſwyke buried.

Hackeney or *Hacquenye*, F. 22. In the church thereof lieth buried, one CHRISTOPHER VRSWYKE whoſe chiefe monument is erected of white free ſtone, in the north ſide of the Chauncell, yet was he interred in the middle of the ſame Chauncell, couered with a faire graie Marble ſtone, pictured in braſſe with this ſubſcription.

CHRISTOPHERVS VRSVVICVS *Regis* HENRICI *ſeptimi Elimoſinarius; vir ſua ætate clarus, ſummantibus atq̃, intimatibus charus, Ad exteros reges undecies pro patria legatus, Deconatum* Eborum *Archidiaconatū* Richmondiæ, *Deconatū* Windeſoriæ *habitos, viuens reliquit, Epiſcopatum* Norwicenſem *oblatū recuſauit* : *Magnos honores, tota vita ſpreuit: frugali vita contentus, hic viuere, hic mori maluit: plenus annis obijt, ab omnibus deſideratus, funeris pompam, etiam teſtamento vetuit: hic ſepultus, carnis reſurectionem, in aduentum Chriſti expectat: obijt Anno Dommini* 1521. 24, *die Octobr.*

The men of our time, who more greedelie thirſt for high and great preferments, then for the diligent execution of their callings, and feeding of Gods people; may by this godly mans example be mooued, ſomthing to morteſie their greedy affections, and enioying onely a ſufficient portion, to endeuour rather the building of the Church of God then their owne glory, And in time to caſt away thoſe things that hinder their going one, in a ſincere courſe of life.

Earle of Northumberland.

In the ſame chauncell is the coat armour, ſhild garter and creſt of the Earle of Northumberland.

The Lady Latymer buried.

In the Church in the north Ile thereof is rayſed a moſt faire and famous monument of Marble and Alablaſter, very curiouſlie contriued, whereon lyeth very neatly figured, the picture and corporall proportion, of the Lady *Lucy*, daughter to the Earle of *Worceſter*, wife vnto ſir *Iohn Neuell* knight Lord *Latymer*, who deceaſed at his mannour of *Snape* in *Yorkeſhire*. The ſaid Lady deceaſed *Anno* 1582. hauing iſſue, foure daughters, *Katherine* the eldeſt maried *Henry* Earle of *Northumberland*, who by her had iſſue *Henry* Lord *Percie*, *Thomas*, *William Charles*, *Richard*, *Allyn*, *Ioſſalyne* and *George*, Lady *Iane*, *Lucy*, and *Elinor*.

Dorathy the ſecond daughter maried ſir *Thomas Cecill* knight, who by hir had iſſue *William*, *Richard*, *Edward*, *Chriſtopher*, and *Thomas*, *Katherine*, *Lucy*, *Myldred*, *Mary*, *Suſan*, *Elizabeth*, *Dorathy*, and *Frances*.

Lucy the third daughter maried *William Cornwallys* Eſquire by whom ſhe had iſſue, *Thomas* and *Iohn*, *Ione*, *Frances*, *Elizabeth*, and *Katherine*.

Elizabeth

Elizabeth the firſt and youngeſt daughter maried ſir *Iohn Danuers* knight, by whom ſhe had iſſue *Charles* and *Henry*, *Anne*, *Lucy*, *Elienor*, and *Mary*.

One   *Heron* Eſquire founded *Hacquenie* Church, and lyeth buried in the north Ile, in a toombe of white free ſtone his armes appeare ingrauen in ſtone in euery piller of the ſame Church thus,

Heron Eſquire buried.

In the ſame Church in the ſouth Ile was buried   *Roe* knight, ſometime Mayor of *London*, his monument is of marble and Alablaſter.

Roe Alderman buried.

Hamerſmith, G. 16.

Hamerſmith hoſpitall, G. 16.

Harlington, G. 8.

Harmeſwoorth, or *Harmundeſwoorth*, G. 6.

Heſton, H. 10. a moſt fertyle place of wheate yet not ſo much to be commended for the quantitie, as for the qualitie, for the wheat is moſt pure, accompted the pureſt in manie ſhires. And therefore Queene E L I Z A B E T H hath the moſt part of her proviſion from that place for manchet for her Highnes owne diet, as is reported.

Hounſlow or *Hunſlow*, H. 10. belongeth vnto two pariſhes, the north ſide of the ſtreete to *Heſton*, and the ſouth to *Iſtlewoorth*: But there is a chappell of eaſe, which belonged vnto the fryerie there diſſolued, which friery after the diſſolutiõ was by exchange giuen to the Lord *Windſore*, by King *Henry* the eight. Afterwardes it came to Auditor *Roan* by purchaſe who hath beſtowed theſame chappell, and 40. ſhillings *per annum* vpon the inhabitantes to the ende and vpon condition that they by farther contribution ſhall maintaine a miniſter there.

* There is a faire houſe erected where the friery was: belonging to the heires of Auditor *Roan*.

In the chappell was buried ſir *George Windſore* knight in a monument of white free ſtone, rayſed with foure pillers. In that place lie many other of the *Windſores*.

Sir George Windſore buried.

Hanworth I. 10. a houſe of hir Maieſties.

Hampton Court K. 12. an honour of Queene E L I Z A B E T H E S, a moſt regall pallace ſtately rayſed of bricke after a moſt princely forme, by Cardinall W O V L S E Y moſt pleaſantly, ſcytuate vpon delightſome *Thamiſe*. Queene E L I Z A B E T H hath of late cauſed

A fountaine erected at Hampton-court.

a very bewtifull fountaine, there to be erected, in the second court which graceth the pallace, and serueth to great and necessarie vse, the fountaine was finished in *Anno* 1590. not without great charge.

Hampton Court why so called.

It is called *Hampton Court* of the parish of *Hampton*, which standeth not far thence: and *Court* commeth of *Curia*, which was the place where the *Senate* of *Rome* assembled, and was taken for the *Senate* it selfe, And thereof groweth our word *Court*, which signifieth all assemblies either for tryall of controuersies, or consulting of matters of state, as also it is amongst vs vsed as an adiunct, to diuers houses in this land of greatest antiquitie, as the most auncient house in a mannor called the *Court house*. But this word *Court* is hereunto added neither in regard of antiquitie, nor head house of a mannor. But in regard of the Maiestie and Princely bewtie thereof, fit for none but for a King or Queene, whose residence in any place draweth a Princely assembly, which is called the *Court*, for where hir Maiesty is resident there is the Court of state. This word Court is a most common adiunct to places of antiquitie in *Artetia*, as also in diuers prouinces of *France* and else where as *Haplincourt*, in *Normandy*, *Bonlayn Court* in *Champaigne*, and *Hallcourt* neere *Amyens*.

Parkes at Hampton Court.

There are belonging to this princely pallace two parkes, the one of Deare, the other of hares, both inuironed with wals of bricke, the south side of the Deare parke, excepted, which is paled and inuironed with the *Thamise*.

Hampton K. 12.

Hanuerde or *Hanforde* K. 8.

I.

Ickenham E· 6.

Islington or *Iseldon* E. 20. belonging to a prebend of *Paules*.

S. Ieames G. 18. hir Maiesties, a very stately house, built after a quadranguler forme, by the famous King *Henry* the eight.

K.

Kyckesende B. 16.

Kingsland E. 20.

Kentishtowne E. 18.

Kylbourne why so called.

Kylbourne or *Keelebourne*, E. 16. seemeth to take name of Keele, and bouŋn which signifie colde water: It is called in some records *Kullebourne*. In the time of *H.* the 1. *Herbert* abbot of *Westminster*, by permission of *Gylbert* byshop of *London*, and by consent of the conuent, graunted to 3. Maides the Hermitage there which one *Gorbone* builded, with all the lande of that place.

Kingesburie, E. 12.

Kenton

Kenton, E. 10.

Knightesbridge, G. 18.

Kensington, G. 16.

Kingstonwyke, K. 14. It is a Hamlet neere *Kingstone* vpon *Thamis*, standing in MYDDLESEX, and is so called, for that it is a rowe *Wike whence* of houses leading into *Kingstone*, which rowe of houses in Lattine *deriued*. is called *Vicus*, in our toong *Vyke* or *Wyke*, of the Saxons pyc. *Vadianus* an excellent Geographer, saith that *Vicus in opido via est* *Vadian Cosmo*. *domorum seriem complexa*, *Vike* is a way or passage in a towne being orderly compact of houses, which we also cal a streete. In *Rome* are divers of these streetes, as *Vicus affricus*, *Vicus ciprius*, & *Vicus celeratus*, *Vicus sceleratus Roma*.

Kenton, K. 10.

L.

London, F. 20. the most famous Citie in all *Brytaine*, which *Erasmus* vpon the Proverbe *Rhodii sacrificium*, saith, is deducted of *Lindus* a citie of the Ile of *Rhodes*, *Stephanus* calleth it *Lyndonium*, the Saxons Lonꝺenꞃeaꞃten, Lonꝺenbiꞃyᵹ Lonꝺenpyc, *Ptolomey*, *Cornelius Tacitus*, and *Antonius*, *Londiniũ*, and *Longidinium*, *Amianus Londinum*: the Welchmen *Lundayne*, we call it *London*: *Ieffrey* of *Monmouth*, *Troia noua*, or *Ternouantum* Newe Troy; some call it *Luddes-Towne* of *Ludde* the eldest sonne of *Helie*: *Leland* taketh it to be *Trenouant*, new Towne, for that in the british toong *Tre* signifieth a towne: M. *Camden* seemeth, in some sort, to yeelde that it should be called *London* of the British word *Lhwn*, which signifieth a woode, or else he will haue it *London* or *Londinum* of the British word *Lhong*, which signifieth ships or shipping, in regarde that our *Thamis* yeeldeth such apt accesse for ships euen to the citie.

There is great varietie among writers, who first founded this Citie: Some will haue *Brute* the Troian to be first builder of it, but *Brute*, and his historie, is meerely reiected of manie in our daies. It was reedefied by *Lud*, in the yeere of the worlds creation 5131. *Bale*. who builded the wals about it, and erected *Ludgate*, who also changed the name of *Trenouant* into *Luddestowne*, now *London*, for which alteration of *Troye* to *Luddestowne*, great contention arose a- *Gildas*. mong the *Britons*, as reporteth *Gildas* and others. But our *Galfrid. Monuni*. late writers will not consent heereunto: Insomuch as this fa- *ponticus Brit. hist*. mous Citie lacketh the truth of it foundation, as many other *lib. 1*. famous monuments also do. But it nowe reteineth the name of *London*, famous through the whole worlde. A Citie of great Marchandize, populous, rich, and beautifull;

This Citie was burned and greatly wasted by the host of the *Greg. in past*. pagan *Danes*, in the time of king *Alphred*, as reporteth *Gregory* in *London burned*.

E 2   his

London reede-fied.

his Paſtorale about the yeere of Chriſt 872. This *Alphred* about the yeere 886.in the 35.yeere of his natiuitie reedefied this Citie, beautifieng the ſame with faire buildings, and committed the cuſtody thereof to *Alphred* Earle of *Mercia*, as the ſame *Gregorie* reporteth.

Fabyan.

A great part of *London* was againe burned about the yeere of Chriſt 981. At what time it had moſt buildings, from *Ludgate* towards *Weſtminſter*, and little, where the heart of the Citie nowe is, but buildings ſcattered heere and there out of forme and order: So that it ſeemed inferior to diuers other Cities of this land, as *Lincolne*, *Canterbury*, *Yorke* and others, as by the role of *Wincheſter* appeereth. But after the conqueſt it was reedefied, and by the conquerour greatly increaſed, So that by degrees it is become a moſt ample and ſtately Citie, far excelling all other in this land.

The gouernement of London.

This Citie was (before the conqueſt)made by *William* Duke of *Normandy*) gouerned by *Portreeues*, called of the Saxons pop-ꞇᵹeꞃeꝼaꞃ whom the Germans call *Burgreues*, which gouernement *Richard* the firſt altered,and appointed two baylifes. Who in the time of King *Iohn* and by his command were diſcharged, for a time, by 35. elders or heads of the Citie, for a contempt againſt the King. But they were not long in diſgrace, but through their ſubmiſſion and the diſcreete handling of the matter by theſe 35. heads or elders of the Citie, the King not onely forgaue the baylifes, but granted vnto the Citie by his letters pattents, that they ſhould yeerely chooſe vnto themſelues, a Mayor which vſually is of one of the 12. companies, mentioned in the Map of the Citie, and two Shirifes who haue beene accuſtomed to take their oth vpon Saint *Mathewes* day, nine daies befor Michelmas, and vpon Michelmas day to take their charge, but it is now otherwiſe.

The firſt Mayor of Lodnon.

The firſt Mayor was choſen in the tenth yeere of King *Iohn*, *Anno* 1209. Euery Mayor was wont to be preſented to the King whereſoeuer he was in *England*, vntill *Henrie* the thirds time, about *Anno* 1242. and before the King to be ſworne; after that it was referred to the Barons of the *Exchequere*, and ſo continueth to this day. Sir *Iohn Allin* knight, twice Mayor of London gaue a coller of gold to be ſucceſſiuely worne by the Mayor *Anno* 1544. In the time of *H*. 3. alſo the Aldermen of the Citie were ordeined, who tooke rule of the particuler wardes thereof,25. in number, and theſe Aldermen were yeerely changed as are the Shirifes, but now it is otherwiſe, which wardes and the pariſhes in them are theſe.

Aldermen of London.

Tower ward.
{ *S. Olaſe.*
{ *Alhallowes* at Berking.
{ *S. Dunſtane.*

Billingſgate

Billingsgate warde.
{
S. *Botolph.*
S. *George* in pudding lane.
S. *Androw* in Eastcheape.
S. *Margaret Passens.*
S. *Mary hill.*
}

Dowgate warde.
{
S. *Laurance Pountney.*
Alhallowes the more.
Alhallowes the lesse.
}

Bridgestreete warde.
{
S. *Bennet* of grace Church.
S. *Leonard* in Eastcheape.
S. *Margaret* in Bridgestreete.
S. *Magnes* in Bridgestreete.
}   } *Newfishstreett.*

Walbrooke warde.
{
S. *Iohn* in Walbrooke.
S. *Mary B.*
S. *Swythyn* in Candlewikestreet.
S. *Stephen* in Walbrooke.
S. *Mary Woulchurch* in the Poultrie.
S. *Syth* in Bucklersbury.
}

Candlewike-streete warde.
{
S. *Martyn Orgor.*
S. *Clement.*
S. *Michael* in Croked lane.
S. *Mary Abchurch.*
}

Langburne warde.
{
Alhallowes Stains in Lumbarestreet.
S. *Gabriell.*
S. *Dionis* in Fanchurch streete.
S. *Edmund.*
S. *Nicholas Acon.*
S. *Mary Wolnosh* in Lumbare streete.
}

Algate ward.
{
S. *Androwes Vndershaft.*
S. *Katherines* by Christeschurch.
S. *Katherin Colman.*
}

Port Sowkin warde.
{
S. *Botolph* without Algate.
}

Lymestreete warde.
{
S. *Mary Nam.*
}

Bishops.

Bufhopes
gate warde.
{
- S. *Botolph* at the gate.
- S. *Alborgth.*
- *Alhallowes* within S. *Helines.*

Cornehill
warde.
{
- S. *Michaell.*
- S. *Peter.*

Brodeftreete
warde.
{
- S. *Martyn Outwich.*
- S. *Bennet Finck.*
- S. *Bartholmew* the little.
- S. *Chriftopher.*
- S. *Peter* the poore.
- *Alhallowes* on the wall.

Colman-
ftreet ward.
{
- S. *Sthephen.*
- S. *Olafe* in the Iurie.
- S. *Margaret* in Lothburie.

Cheape
warde.
{
- S. *Laurence* in the Iurie.
- S. *Marie Bow.*
- *Alhallowes* in hony lane.
- S. *Marie* of *Colchurch.*
- S. *Myldreds* in the Pultrie.
- S. *Bennet Shorehog.*
- S. *Martyn Poniers,*
- S. *Martyn* in Iremonger lane.
- S. *Maryes.*

Ordwayner
ftrek warde
{
- S. *Marie* or *Aldermarie.*
- S. *Anceline.*
- S. *Pancras.*

Queenehyth
warde.
{
- S. *Mychaell.*
- S. *Mary Somerfet.*
- S. *Mary Mowfhaw.*
- S. *Nicholas Olafe.*
- S. *Nicholas* colde Abbey.
- S. *Peter.*

Bredftreete
warde.
{
- *Alhallowes* in Bredftreete.
- S. *Myldred.*
- S. *Mathie.*
- S. *Io. Euangelift.*
- S. *Auguftine* at Paules gate.

                            S. *Margaret*

S. *Margaret Moyses.*
S. *Botolph.*
S. *Margaret* in Friday ſtreete.

Vintry warde.
S. *Martyn.*
S. *Mychaell Colledge.*
S. *Thomas Apoſtle.*
S. *Iames* on Garlikehyth.
Trinitie in Knightriderſtreete.

Beynerdca-ſtle warde.
S. *Andrew.*
S. *Bennet.*
S. *George.*
S. *Mary Magdelene* in old fiſhſtreete.

The warde of Farringdon *infrd.*
S. *Euan.*
S. *Nicholas* in the Fleſhſhambles.
S. *Faithes* in Paules.
S. *Martyn* within Ludgate.
S. *Mychaell* at *Querne.*
S. *Fauſter* in Fauſter lane.
S. *Peter* at the croſſe of Cheape.
S. *Gregory* in Paules Churchyarde.
S. *Genyn* within S. Martin *le graunde.*

The warde of Farringdon *extra.*
S. *Dunſtane.*
S. *Bride.*
S. *Androw* in Holborne.
S. *Pulcher* without Newgate.

Aldreſgate-ſtreet warde.
S. *Botolph* without Aldreſgate.
S. *Anne.*
S. *Iohn Zacharie.*
S. *Leonard* in Fauſter lane.
S. *Marie Staining.*
S. *Mathew* in ſiluer ſtreete.

Baſſinghall warde.
S. *Mychaell.*

Creplegate warde.
S. *Mary Magdelene.*
S. *Marie* in Aldermanburie.
S. *Michaell* in Hogginlane.
S. *Albons* in Woodſtreete.
Elſinge ſpittle now a pariſh church.

S. *Olofe*

⌠ S. *Olafe* in Syluerſtreete.
⌊ S. *Gyles* without the gate.

Wardes 25.
Pariſhes.113.

Other Churches there are within this Citie not mentioned in
the wardes, nor vſed as pariſh Churches : whereof the firſt is
Paules *buylded.*   *Paules,* a moſt ſtately temple, builded by *Ethelbert* king of *Kent,an-*
*no,*610. who conſecrated the ſame vnto S. *Paule.* It was afterward
augmented by *Mauricius* biſhop of *London, anno* 1107. *Henry Lacy*
Earle of Lincolne, builded the ſouth croſſe Ile, & was there buried
anno 1310. It is a Cathedrall Church the biſhops Sea of *London;*
ſometime the archbiſhops Sea, but remooued thence to *Caunter-*
burie, by the meanes of S. *Auguſtine,* at the requeſt of the Citizens
Paules *ſteeple.*   of *Caunterbury.* In the middell of this famous temple, is a Tower
moſt artificially raiſed vpon ſtrong pillers, verie admirable to be
conſidered, for that the foundation of the ſame maine Tower can
not be deſerned in the bodie of the Church, and yet aſcendeth in
great altitude, as it were in the center of the church, not (without
curious view) to be ſeene, howe it is ſupported : vpon this Tower
was raiſed a *Piramis* or (as we cōmonly terme it) a Steeple, couered with lead, which is ſaide to haue beene in altitude equall with
the church in longitude, the height therof is recorded to be 534.
Paules *ſteeple*   foote from the ground: which ſtately *piramis* or ſteeple was thrice
burned three   conſumed with fire: firſt in the yeere of Chriſt 1087. which was
times.   not long after newlie erected: and burned againe *anno* 1444. after
that raiſed and againe conſumed with fire, by vnknowne meanes
(the iudgement of God inkindling it) in the yeere of Chriſt 1561.
to the terror of the whole Citie : remaining as yet wihtout that
ſtately ornament.

Sebba *buried.*   There lieth buried *Sebba* king of the eaſt
Saxons who died *anno domini* 633. in a coffin
of marble with couer of the ſame, his armes
theſe.

King **Etheldred**   There alſo lieth buried *Etheldred* king
buried.   of *England,* the ſonne of *Edgar* who died *an-*
no domini 1017. in a coffin of marble with couer of the ſame.

Io.Plantaginet   There lieth alſo *Iohn* ſurnamed *Plantaginet*
buried.   in a ſtately monument, artificially raiſed of white free ſtone,
whoſe ſtile is thus there recorded.

Illuſtriſſimus iacet hic, Iohannes *cognomento* Plantaginet, *Rex* Ca-
ſtiliæ, *&* Legionis, *Dux* Lancaſtrie, *Comes* Richmondiæ Le-
ceſtriæ, Lincolnie *&* Derbiæ, *locum tenens* Aquitaniæ , *magnus*
Seneſcallus

Senefcallus Angliæ *obiit anno* 22.Ric.2. *Annoque Domini* 1399.

Alſo there was a Church at the *Crotched fryars* now conuerted to other vſe.

A Church at *Auguſtine friars* founded by *Humfrey Bohune* E. of *Hertford*, 1253.

A Church called *Tho.* of *Acris* neer the great conduct in *Cheape* founded by *Thomas fitz Theobald* in the time of H. 2. who gaue the ſame Church to the *Mercers* for a peece of money, at the ſuite of ſir *Richard Greſham* knight, and is now vſed for the *Mercers hall*. Rec. E.3. Anno 19.

The *Temple* within *Temple barre*, whoſe founder is not certainely recorded, yet ſome hold it to be that which was called *Templum pacis* or *Concordiæ*, builded by *Dunwallo Mulmutius*, about the yeer of the worldes creation 4748. and therein was buried the ſame *Mulmutius* and alſo *Gorbomanus* and others. But ſome take the *Temple* of peace to be that which is now *Blackwell-hall*. There are in this *Temple*, many very auncient monuments of famous men, ſhaped in Marble armed, their legges croſſe, whoſe names are not to be gathered, by any inſcription, for that, time hath worne it out. The form of this *Temple*, in the weſt, is made circuler, loftely raiſed with Marble pillers, ſet alſo circulerly, ſo that it ſerueth, the ſtudents of the houſe for a walke moſt neceſſarie, & that, for a multitude without diſturbance of one by the other, by reuerting. Some ſay it was founded by the kings templers which were in *England* about the yeere of Chriſt 1185. but it ſeemeth that this *Temple* is farre more auncient. The Temple.

Galfr. Mon.

There was annexed vnto the *Stilliarde* an auncient Church called the *Temple* alſo, and after the diſſolution thereof, it was giuen to the ſtudents of the Law, bearing the name of *White hall*, which belike in regard of the diſtance from the other houſes of Law, it was at the length neglected and forſaken, which houſe ſeemeth to be of the number of the houſes of Chauncery, in the time of *Henry* the ſixt, when Maſter *Forteſcue* compiled his booke of the Lawes of *England*, wherein he affirmeth that there were in, and neere *London*, ten Innes of Chauncery, now but eight, in which number of ten, was accompted this *White hall*, & the *Strand* Inne, which ſtood within the compaſſe of *Somerſet houſe* neere the *Strand*. A Temple neere the Stilliarde.

White hall.

The *Stilliarde* (called of the *Gothes* the *Haunſe*) ſignifieth a place of meeting of the people, and eſpecially the Marchants of many Countries, and Cities: as of *England*, *France*, *Denmarke*, *Muſcouie*, *Brabant*, *Flaunders*, and many other, where they enterchanged Marchandize by the ſundry priuileges and freedomes of many Kings, Dukes, and Princes, which of late yeeres hath by little and little diſcontinued. It is not againſt reaſon, to thinke that theſe auncient *Temples* were erected by the *Pagans* wherein they offe Stilliarde why ſo called.

F   red

Galfr.Mon.

red facrifices to their countrey gods. For it appeareth by the hi-
ftorie of *Ieffery* of *Monmoth* that while *C. Alectus* Captaine of the
Romaine hoft, was thus bufied in his Pagan facrifice M. *Aur. Afclepiodotus* duke of *Cornewall* whom the *Britons* had elected to be
their King, came to *London*, and befieged, and entred it ; betweene
whom was a hard conflict and *Afclepiodotus* vanquifhed the *Romanes* and after befet *Gallus* another Captaine of the *Romanes*
who remained in the citie, and ouercame him, who with his *Romanes* being put to the fworde the chiefe Captaine *Gallus* was caft
into a brooke, which then, and long fince, ran through the Citie,

Walbrooke.

whereof it is fuppofed to be called of the auncient *Britons*, *Nants-
gall* of the *Saxons* ʒalenbouɲne, and of vs at this day *Wallbrooke*,
which runneth neere *London ftone* which ftone is neere in the mid
way betweene *Ludd gate* and the Tower pofterne gate.

    There are about this Citie 11. Gates of name, whereof foure
are towardes the north, as *Alderfgate* fuppofed to be fo called of
the *Alders* which grew there, and fome holde it to take name of
Aldricius the *Saxon*, it may be fo called of the antiquitie thereof,
Aldeftgate in the comparatiue degree as *Aldgate*, *Newgate*, in the
pofitiue. *Creplegat*, So called for that it was the houfe for halt and
lame, a hofpitall for creeples and impotent people, it hath beene
of late reedified by *Edmond Thaa* in the yeere of Chrift 1490.
Moregate fo called for that it was the paffage into a moorifh, me-
rifh, or watrie ground, which is called *Moore fielde*, though now
brought to be more firme, by the induftry and charge of a Mayor
of *London* about 180.yeeres paft. *Bufhopes gate* builded by certaine
Marchantes which traueled into *Germaine* belonging to the olde
Haunce : But it feemeth by the adiunct that it fhould be builded
by a Bufhop.

    There are vpon the *Thamis* three gates, though two of them
feeme rather portes or hauens for fhipes and boates then gates
for paffage, onely the *Bridge gate* is a thorough fare, or paffage by
horfe and foote, but *Billingfgate* is a harbor or kaye for fhipping, yet

Galfr. Mon.

hath the name of a gate, for that it was erected firft like a gate,
by *Bellinus*, and of him called *Bellines gate*, in the top whereof he
caufed to be erected a *Pyramis* and on the top of it a veffell of
ftone, wherein he appointed the afhes of his brent body to be put
after his death. There is alfo *Dowgate* or *Dourgate* that is *Watergate*

    On the eaft is one gate called *Aldegate*, fo called of the antiqui-
tie thereof, as M. *Camden* and others fuppofe.

    On the weft are two gates *Luddgate* or *Luddefgate*, of L v D D the
fuppofed founder, who is faide to lie interred in the Church of S.

*Anno ante Chrif-
tum 66.*

Martins within the gate. This gate was of late yeeres newly builded and made a moft ftately gate about the yeere of Chrift, 1586.

Galfr.Mon.

to the great charge of the Citie. *Ieffrey* of *Monmouth* reporteth,
that

that the image of C A D W A L L O was in braſſe artificially fixed on Cadwallo *buried*
a braſen horſe,ſet on the toppe of this gate, in token of a victorie
had againſt the *Saxons* : whoſe body was alſo buried in S. *Martynes*
church within the gate.

There was betweene *London* and *Southwarke* long time paſſage *London bridge* .
by ferrie vntill the Citizens cauſed a bridge of woode to be erected : after that, in the time of R I C. 2. *anno* 1176. they beganne to
build a bridge of ſtone, which in the time of king I O H N they moſt
artificially finiſhed, *anno* 1209. contriuing it of 20. arches, and in
the midſt a drawe bridge, and vppon the ſame bridge on either
ſide, the houſes ſo artificially combined, that the whole bridge
ſeemeth not onely a mayne and faire ſtreete, but men ſeeme to
paſſe vnder a continuall roofe; the bridge is in height 60. foote,
in bredth 30. foote, the arches are in ſunder 20. foote, there are vnder the north arch of this bridge, moſt artificially erected certain
wheeles or tide myles, which riſe and fall according to the ebs &
flouds, and they raiſe the water by pypes and counductes ſo high
that it ſerueth ſuch citizens houſes in all places of *London*, as will
beſtow charge towarde the conducting thereof : The buildings *Pollid, Virg.*
vppon this bridge, on either ſide were conſumed with fire *Anno* 1208.

There is neere the three Cranes, a Church called now S. *Mi-
chaels*, ſometime *Whittingdon Colledge* founded by ſir   *Whit-* *Whit-*
tingdon, ſometime Mayor of *London*.

There was in that place which is nowe knowne by the name of Fitzſtephanus
Blacke-fryers, an auncient and ſtrong caſtle, which was called *Pa-* Palatine.
latyne, burned in the time of W I L L I A M the *Conquerour* : in the
place of which caſtle are at this day erected many faire & beautifull buildings, and here and there the auncient wals and buildings as yet appeare.

On the eaſt part of the Citie, is a moſt famous and ſtrong Caſtle, called the *Tower of London*, the maine tower whereof, ſome ſup- The Tower.
poſe to be builded by I V L I V S C AE S A R. It is ſtrong and ample,
well walled and trenched about, beautified with ſundrie build-
dings, ſemblable to a little towne.

There is in *Cornehill* a moſt famous monument, ſtately erected
by ſir *Thomas Greſham* knight, who named it the *Burſe*, whereunto The Royall Ex-
afterwarde Queene E L I Z A B E T H gaue the name of *Royall ex-* change.
change; It is the place of the publike meeting of Marchaunts,
aſwell Engliſh as foraine, wherunto twice euery day they dulie re-
ſort, the form of the building is quadrate, with walks round the
mayne building ſupported with pillers of marble, ouer which
walkes is a place for the ſale of all kinde of wares, richly ſtored
with varietie of all ſorts. It was builded about the yeere 1568.

Leaden hall neere *Cornhill* was builded by one *Sunken Eyre*, about Leaden hal'.

F 2 anno

anno 1444. a place of prouifion, or ftore houfe for releefe for the poore in time of dearth.

Manie things might be fpoken of this famous Citie which would too far exceede my purpofe. It hath latitude 52.degrees,& longitude 19.degrees 15.minuts. It is moft fweetely fcituate vpon the *Thamis*, ferued with all kinde of neceffaries moft commodiouflie. The aire healthfull,it is populous, rich and beautifull;be it alfo faithfull, louing and thankfull.

Lodghill D. 16. a hill or fort in *Harnefey* or *Hornefey* parke, and is called *Lodghill*, for that thereon fometime ftoode a lodge, when the parke was replenifhed with Deare, but it feemeth by the foundation that it was rather a caftle, then a lodge, for the hill is at this day trenched with two deepe ditches, now olde and ouergrowne with bufhes :the rubble thereof, as bricke,tile, and Cornifh flate,are in heapes yet to be feene, which ruines are of great antiquity,as may appeere by the okes,at this day ftanding(aboue 100.yeeres grouth,)vpon the very foundation of the building.It did belong to the bifhop of *London*, at which place haue beene dated diuers euidences,fome of which remaine yet in the bifhops regeftrie(as is faid.)

This parke hath beene replenifhed with ftately timber trees in great aboundance,now with the famous fort fallen to the ground as the Poet faith,

> *Euum cuncta rapit furtiuáque tempora mutant.*
>
> *Naturam, fortem, Nomináque & faciem.*

* * *Ludgraues*, B.18.a faire houfe feytuate in a valley neere *Enfeylde* chace,belonging vnto

Lymehoufe, G.22.

Lalam, I.8.

Littleto n I.8.in regard of the quantitie it may be called *Littletowne.*

M.

More hall,E.4.

Mylhill,D.14.

Mufwell hill,D. 18.called alfo *Pinfenall hill :* there was a chapple fometime bearing the name of our Ladie of *Mufwell :* where now alderman *Roe* hath erected a proper houfe, the place taketh name of the Well and of the hill, *Moufewell hill*, for there is on the hil a fpring of faire water, which is now within the compas of the houfe. There was fometime an image of the ladie of *Mufwell*, whereunto was a continuall refort, in the way of pylgrimage, growing as is (though as I take it)fabuloufliereported,in regard of a great cure which was performed by this water, vpon a king of

of *Scots*,who being ſtrangely diſeaſed,was by ſome deuine intelli-
gence,aduiſed to take the water of a Well in *England*,called *Muſ-
well*, which after long ſcrutation, and inquiſition , this Well was
found and performed the cure; abſolutely to denie the cure I
dare not,for that the high God hath giuen vertue vnto waters, to
heale infirmities, as may appeere by the cure of *Naaman* the le-
per,by waſhing himſelfe ſeauen times in *Iordan*, and by the poole **2. King.1.14.**
Betheſda,which healed the next that ſtepped thereinto, after the **Iohn 5.2.**
water was mooued by the angell.

* *Mockings*, called alſo the mannor of *Mockings*, D.22. an auncient houſe, of the Lord *Comptons*,moated about.

Morehatch,A. 20.a hamlet of *Enfeylde*.

Marybone,F.18.

Meerſtreete, F.22. a member of *Hackney*.

N.

Northend,C. 16.a hamlet of *Finchley*.

** *Newington*,E.20.there, the Earle of *Oxforde* is ſometime reſident,in a very proper houſe.

Newington greene,E.20.

** *Neeſdon*,or *Neuſdon*,E.14.a houſe ſometime the *Elringtons*.

Northolt lodge,F.6.

Northolt, F.8.it ſoundeth *Northwood*, for *holt* in the Germayne
toung ſignifieth wood.

Norwood,or *Northwood*,F.8.

Norcote,or *Northcote*,G.8.

O.

Olde forde, F. 22. a village taking name of the forde or paſſage
at that place, ouer the riuer *Lea* in time paſt.

* *Oſterley*, or *Oyſterley*, G. 10. the houſe nowe of the ladie *Greſ- **Oſterley builded.***
hams*,a faire and ſtately building of bricke, erected by ſir *Thomas
Greſham* knight,Citizen and Marchant aduenturer of *London*, and
finiſhed about *anno* 1577. It ſtandeth in a parke by him alſo im-
paled, well wooded,and garniſhed with manie faire ponds, which
affoorded not onely fiſh, and fowle , as ſwanes, and other water
foule:but alſo great vſe for milles,as paper milles,oyle milles,and
corne milles,all which are now decaied (a corne mill excepted.)
In the ſame parke was a verie faire Heronrie , for the increaſe &
preſeruation whereof, ſundrie allurements were deuiſed and ſet
vp fallen all to ruine.

P.

Pynner,E.8.

*Pymmes,

Pymmes, C.20. a proper little houſe of the right Honorable Lord *Burghley*, Lord high *Treaſurer* of *England*.

Ponders end, B.20. a hamlet of *Enſeylde*.

Potters bar, A.16.

Preſton, E.12.

Peryuale, or *Pureuale*, F.10. of this place is ſpoken before in the nature of the ſoyle of MYDDLESEX.

Paddington, F.16.

Paddingwyke, G.14. for the the ſignification of Wyke ſee *Kingſtonwyke*.

Pancras Church very auncient.

Pancras Church, F.20.) ſtandeth all alone as vtterly forſaken, old and wetherbeaten, which for the antiquitie thereof, it is thought not to yeeld to *Paules* in *London*: about this Church haue bin manie buildings, now decaied, leauing poore *Pancras* without companie or comfort: yet it is now and then viſited with *Kentiſh towne* and *Highgate*, which are members therof: but they ſeldome come there, for that they haue chappels of eaſe within themſelues, but when there is a corps to be interred, they are forced to leaue the ſame in this forſaken church or churchyard, where (no doubt) it reſteth as ſecure againſt the day of reſurrection as if it laie in ſtately *Paules*.

Pancras as deſſolate as it ſtandeth is not forſaken of all: a prebrend of *Paules* accepeth it in right of his office.

Parſons greene, H.16.

R.

Riſe lip E. 16.

S.

Syon builded.

Syon, H. 12. was built by HENRIE the 5. ſometimes a houſe of munkes, but this king expelled them, and in their place eſtabliſhed certaine virgins of *Bridgets* order; and appointed of them ſo many with prieſts and lay brethren, as were equall with the number of the Apoſtles and Diſciples of Chriſt, namelie of virgines 60. prieſts 13. deanes, 4. lay brethren 8. which made 13. Apoſtles, and 72. Diſciples of Chriſt, vpon whome hauing beſtowed ſufficient reuenues for their maintenaunce, he made a lawe that they ſhould not accept of any other gift, but content themſelues with his contribution: and to beſtow on the poore whatſoeuer was aboue that which might reaſonably ſuffice them.

It is now a houſe of hir Maieſties, ſtanding moſt pleaſantly vpon the riuer of *Thamys*. It was called *Syon* in remembrance of that hill in *Ieruſalem*, which was called the *Holy hill*, the *mount of the Lord*, the

the *Citie of Dauid, Mount Syon*.

** *Swakeleys*, E. 6. fometime a houfe of the *Brockeyes*, nowe fir *Thomas Sherleyes*.

Stanmer great, D. 10.

Stanmer little, called alfo *Whytechurch*, D. 10.

South mymmes, A. 14. there is a faire warren of conies of the Lo. *Windfores*.

Shackelwell, E. 22.

Shordich, F. 20.

Stretford on the bow, F. 24. the bridge ouer the riuer Lea, is the Bow, and thereof is called *Stratford on the bow*, neere it, is an olde church, founded by H E N. 2. Rec. E. *anno 22*.

Sir Henry Collet knight buried.

Stepney, or *Stybenhyth*, or *Stibonbeath*, F. 22. In the church thereof is buried fir *Henry Collet* knight, twice Mayor of *London*, who was father to *Iohn Collet*, fometime Deane of *Paules*, who alone builded *Paules fchoole*, his armes thefe.

There lyeth alfo the Lady *Anne Wentworth* wife to *Thomas* Lord *Wentworth*, and daughter to *Henry Wentworth* Efquier. She died the fecond of Sept. 1571.

Stepney. Lady Wentworth *buried*.

Sir *Thomas Spert* knight fometime Controler of the fhipes to H. 8. Dame *Margery*, Dame *Anne*, and Dame *Mary* his wiues, lie in the Chauncell there, he deceafed *Anno* 1541.

Sir Thomas Spert *knight buried*.

In

William Chald-nam Efquire buried.

In the north Ile of the fame Church lyeth *William Chaldnâm* efquire, and *Ioan* his wife he died the 27. of Sept. *Anno* 1484.

Strond,called the *Stroud* H.4. a hamlet neere *Chefwyke*,and called the *Strond*, for that it bordereth fo neere the *Thamys*.

Southholt, fignifieth Southwood, G.8.

Sypfon,G.6.

** *Stanwell* H.6. there was the auncient houfe of the *Windfores*.

Stanes Church,H.6.

Stanes towne, I.6. it is called in the *Saxon* toong. � It ftandeth vpon the *Thamis*, A market towne kept on the Friday weekly, it is gouerned by two Cunftables and foure Headborrowes: the towne is hir Maiefties lande, and the officers chofen by hir Highnes Steward. It ftandeth from the church halfe a mile, and the Church ftandeth vppon a little hill by it felfe, at if it were banifhed the towne.

Coway ftakes.

Some affirme it to be called *Stanes* of the Stakes called *Coway Stakes*, which were fixed in the *Thamys* by the Brytons, to preuent *Iulius Cæfar*,of paffing his armie through the riuer. There is a towne called *Stanes* vpon the frontires of Italie in *Tyroll*, vpon

Bunn meadow.

the riuer *Inn*. There is a medow neere *Stanes* called *Bunn meadow*, where king I O H N had parley with his barons, and where were fealed betweene them certeyne writings of truce.

Nicafius Yetf-worth buried.

Sunburye K. 10. *Nicafius Yetfworth* efquire, fometime fecretarie of the French tongue to Queene E L I Z A B E T H: And *Marie* his wife, daughter to *Ieames Bowfer* efquire, lie buried in the fame church.

Daniel Rogers buried.

There was alfo buried *Daniell Rogers* Efquire fometime Clerke of the Counfell to Queene E L I Z A B E T H a man of excellent learning, and knowledge of toongs, and often imploid in Ambaffage into *Germainie, Denmarke, Low Countries, &c.*

Shepperton K. 8.

T.

Tottenham or *Totheham* D. 20. In which Church is buried *George Heningham* efquire fometime feruant, & greatly fauored of K. *Henrie vie* the eight he founded there a little hospitall or almeshouse for three poore widowes.

* At this place the Lord *Compton* hath a proper ancient house.

Tottenham highcrosse D. 20. a hamlet belonging to *Tottenham*, and hath this adiunct *Highcrosse* of a woodden crosse, there loftly raysed on a little mount of earth.

Tottenham streete C. 20.

Twyforde west E. 12. So called of two little brookes or fordes that passe neere it. It is a parish but it hath but one onely house thereunto belonging, which is one *Iohn Lions* Gentleman.

Twyforde east E. 12. belonging to a prebend of Paules.

Totten Court F. 18. belonging to a prebend of Paules.

Turnham greene G. 14.

Thistleworth or *Istleworth* H. 12. a place scytuate vpon the *Thamis*, not far from whence, betweene it and *Worton*, is a copper and brasse mill, where it is wrought out of the oare, melted and forged. The oar, or earth, whereof it is contriued, is brought out of *Sommerset shire* from *Mendip hils*, the most from *Worley hill*, manie artificiall deuises there are to be noted in the performance of the worke.

Copper and brasse

Twickenham I. 12 a parish scytuate vpon the *Thamis*. So called either for that, at that place the *Thames* semeth to be deuided into two Riuers by reason of the Islandes there, or else of the two brookes which neere the towne enter into the *Thamis*, for *Twicknam* is as much as *Twynam*, *quasi inter binos amnes situm*, a place scytuate betweene two riuers.

Twickenham why so called.

Tuddinton I. 12.

V.

Vxbridge or *Woxbridge* F. 4. a market towne vpon the edge of the shire, it is no parish of it selfe, but is a member of great *Hellingdon*, but they haue a Chappell of ease buylt by *Ro. Oliuer, Thomas Mandin, Iohn Palmer,* & *Iohn Barforde* of the same towne. In the six and twentith yeere of *Henry* the sixt. The market is kept on the Thursday. It is gouerned by two Baylifes, two Cunstables, and foure Tythingmen called also Headborrowes, or as the *Saxons* call them Boþheycaloonꝛ the chiefest or head pledges.

Vxenden or *Oxenden* E. 12.

W.

* * *Woodhall* E. 8. the house of
* *Wirehall* E. 20. the house of   *Leeke* Esquire.

Walsham crosse A. 20. The farthest part of this shire towardes

the

the north, goeth to the Spittle there.

Whitweb A.20.

Whetstone C. 16.

Wilsdon of the *Saxons* piuelȝoune E. 14.

Wembly hill E. 12.

West bourne F. 16. West water.

Winchmore hill B. 20.

Westminster G. 18. Sometime called *Thorney* of the *Saxons*

Dorney for Thor- Ꝺopney of some *Dorney* but (as I take it) *D.* is pronounced in
neys steede of *Th.* as it is in many other ancient *Saxon* words, as Fader,
Moder, Broder, for Father, Mother, Brother, which error ariseth
belike of the mistaking of the capitall *D.* abreauiated thus Đ.
which is as much as *Th.* and the little *d.* thus abreuiated ᵭ. for
Th. which abreuiations are often taken for the simple *D.* and d. by
reason whereof it was called Ꝺopney for Đopney.

This *Thorney* now *Westminster* was an Island inuironed with the
*Thamis,*which deuided it selfe, and one braunch passed betweene
Charing crosse and *Kings-streete,* throrowgh S. *Ieames parke* that now
Thorney some- is, including *Tootehill,* and was called *Thorney* Island, for that it
time an Island. was ouergrowen with bryers and thornes; which *Thorney* place
was in the time of King L v c i v s(as Authors affirme)clensed,a
bout the yeere 186. which L v c i v s is saide to lay the first foun-
S. Peters foun- dation of the great Temple of S. *Peters.* But Authors greatly vary
ded. touching the founders of the same Temple. Master *Camden* from
Sulcardus reporteth that there was first a Temple in that place,
dedicate to *Apollo,* which was ouerthrowne by an earth quake in
Galfr. Mon. the time of *Antonius Pius.* It is not vnlike that such an Idol Temple was, for it is reported by auncient Authors, that the *Troyno-*
uantes, or *Trinobantes,* did somtime sacrifice Buls,Bullockes,Stags,
and such like to *Diana Tauropolia* whom the Gentiles called the
Queene of *Heauen.* Of the ruynes of that Idoll Temple,It is said
that S E B E R T V S King of the east *Saxons* erected another Temple for the seruice of the liuing God, and consecrated the same
to S. *Peter,* about the yeere of Christ 610. neere about the time
of the buildiug of *Paules.* Afterwardes it was destroyed by the
Math. Westm. *Danes,* and *Dunstan* Bushop of *London,* reedified it about the yeere
of Christ 960. and made there a monasterie for 12. Munckes.*Fa-*
bian saith it was builded by the means of E T H E L B E R T King-
of *Kent,* who also built *Paules* in *London.*

I haue heard that there are,or haue beene,records in the same
Abbey, which declare that it was a Church before the *Britons* re-
ceiued the faith, of Christ, which should seeme to be that Idoll
Church of *Apollo* before L v c i v s time.

This stately and famous S. *Peters,* hath by degrees come to it
present bewtie, many handes haue been helpers to the finishing
thereof;

thereof; about the yeere of Chrift 950. *Edgar* is faid to haue ad- *Policr.*
Guido.
ded thereunto, then *Dunftane*, After him E DVV A R D the confef- *Virgil.*
for the fonne of *Etheldred* about the yeere 1049. and laftly (as *Fabian.*
Fabian faith) (in fome part agreeing with other Authors) that
H E N R Y the third when he had pulled downe what E DVV A R D
had fet vp, rayfed a more ftatly worke, in the yeere of Chrift 1229.
and finifhed the fame in the yeere 1285. wherein I take *Fabian* to
be deceiued, for by this computation, he argueth that the new
worke of H E N R Y the third was 66. yeeres in building, yet begun S.Peters church
and finifhed, by H E N R Y the third, who raigned but 57. yeeres. 50. *yeeres in buil-*
ding.
Other Authors agree it was 50. yeeres in finifhing.

After *Thorney*, it became to be called *Weftminfter*, and that in
regard of the fcytuation of it weft of *London:* for on the Tower hill
was a monafterie called *Eaftminfter*, of the eafterly ftanding Eaftminfter.
thereof, which was called alfo *New abbey*, founded by E D w. 3.
in the yeee 1359.

There are within this temple, diuers, and fundrie, moft rare
and princely monuments: fome of great antiquitie, fome alfo
of later times, increafing dailie, among the reft there lieth E D- Edward confef-
W A RD called alfo the *Confeffor*, who laboured before in this famous for *buried.*
worke, and caufed his corps to be interred in the weft part of
the Church, which when H E N. 3. had altred, he caufed the body
of E D w. to be remooued, to the place where now it refteth, in the
eaft part of the Church.

Alfo there lieth H E N. 3. the finifher of this moft famous Henry the third
worke, whofe tombe is there in moft kingly manner erected, by *buried.*
Tho.Walfing.
the dutifull endeuour and charge of E D w. 1. fonne of the faid
H E N. 3. and for that purpofe, he brought Iafper ftones out of
Fraunce, wherewith he beautified his fathers fumptuous fepulchre
in *anno* 1280.

Manie other Kings and Queenes, and perfons of high ftate,
haue beene there buried, of whome the whole catalogue to re-
fite would be tedious.

There is in this temple a ftone, in forme of a chaire, fometime *A ftone chayre in*
S.Peters Church
feruing, as the throne of the kings of *Scots*, and wherein they were
crowned, which ftone was brought out of *Scone* in *Scotland* by EDW.
1. fonne to H E N. 3. about *anno* 1297. which ftandeth not far from
his fathers monument, had in no little price at this day.

There is adioining vnto this famous temple, in the eaft ende *A chappell of*
H.7.
thereof, a chappell erected by H E N. 7. which in regarde of the
beautie, and curious contriued worke thereof, is called of *Lelande*,
Orbis miraculum: The wonder of the worlde. In this mirrour of art, *Orbis miraculum.*
and archytect, are many rare and glorious monuments of *Kings*
and Queenes, among whom the famous founder H E N. 7. lieth H.7. *buried.*
vnder a moft regall tombe, framed & artificially formed of bras,
richly

richly guilded with pure gold.

Neere this chappell adioining vnto the *Thamys*, was an olde
famous building, called nowe the *Olde pallace*, which was consu-
med with fire, in the time of E D W. the *Confessor*.

It was sometime the pallace of king C A N V T V S the *Dane*, also
king of *Denmarke*, and where he made his abode about the yeere
of Christ, 1035. after his returne from *Rome* into *Englande*, who
in regard of his quadruplicitie of kingdomes, esteemed himselfe,
more than a man mortall: for his Scicophants had so bewitched
him with their inchaunted flatteries, that he deemed himselfe no
lesse then a God. And in this proud conceit on a day he passed by
the *Thamys*, which ran by that pallace, at the flowing of the tide, &
making staie neere the water, the waues cast foorth some part of
the water towards him, this C A N V T V S coniured the waues by
his regall commaunde to proceede no farther: the *Thamys* vnac-
quainted with this newe God, held on it course, flowing as of cu-
stome it vsed to do, and refrained not to assayle him neere to the
knees: whereat this high conceited man as one amazed, begon
to tremble, starting backe protesting that hee was but a man,
though a mightie king. And that he that gouerned those waters,
was onely worthie to be called a king, and all mortall men, most
mightie kings, ought to subiect them vnto him. A woorthie note
whereby is seene howe the almightie *Iehouah* by his weake creatures, maketh to stoope the most puissant in his owne conceite.
Some part of this old pallace is yet standing, as S. *Stephens chappel*,
and other buildings vpon the *Thamys*, neere vnto which is a most
famous hall, called *Westminster hall*, which was so called for that it
was *Aula regis*, a kings court, but as touching the founder is great
varietie.

Some affirme that W I L L I A M R V F V S builded it: but M.
Camden affirmeth that *Hoc quod nunc habemus pretorim* R I C. 2. *diru-
to vetustiori extruxit suæque habitationi dicauit*. R I C. 2. built it and
made it his mansion house. But me thinks it is to be gathered by
the words of *Thomas Walsingham*, that *Westminster hall* was in the
time of E D W. the 2. where he saith, *Si ipsi Barones cum suis assen-
tatoribus in aula Westmonasterii & pleno parliamento venirent &c.*
whereby it appeereth that *Westminster hall* and the place of par-
lament there, was 64. yeeres before R I C. 2. But some may say,
that the great Hall that nowe is, was not in those daies, but
the Hall that is nowe called *White hall*, where the Court of
of *Requests* is now kept. To answere that the same *Thomas* saith,
Rex E. 1. Celebrauit penticostes in aula magna apud Westmonasterium,
whereby he maketh a distinction betweene those two hals, for
the *White hall* was called also *Aula parua*, the little hall: which two
hals and other buildings thereunto adioining, were vsed by R I C.

the

the 2.who caused all controuersies there to be heard, (who as all other kings)in those daies sat in iudgemēt:& whersoeuer the king was in person, there was the place of hearing, and determining causes: sauing that the common plees were by HEN.3. appointed to be heard in a place certaine, as appeereth in *magna Charta*, where it is saide, *Communia placita non sequntur Curiam nostram. Sed teneantur in aliquo loco certo.* But at this day all causes of whatsoeuer nature, for the most part are heard and determinable, at this place as a place certeine.

Betweene *Westminster hall*, and the *Thamys* is a chapple of S. Stephens: sometime verie beautifull, though now in the outwarde shewe something defaced: It was reedefied and augmented by EDW.3. when he came victor out of *Fraunce*, about the yeere of Christ 1347.

Westminster had sometime a house of monkes, who were remooued thence by HEN.7. and a Deane with certaine Prebends established.

In the time of EDWARD 6. it was made a bishops See, but shortlie after it came againe to a Deane and Prebends; Againe Queene MARIE ordeined there an Abbot and his munkes, who continued not manie yeeres, but were againe cut off by acte of Parleament: Lastly our most gratious Queene ELIZABETH made it a collegiate Church : instituting a Deane, twelue Prebends, twelue well deseruing soldiers, and fortie schollers: who are thereby termed *The Queenes schollers*, who, as they become woorthie, are preferred to the Vniuersities. All which pupils, as long as they continue in this colledge, are vnder the Deane, now D. *Goodman*.

Alexander Neuell Norwic. affirmeth that the Bishops of *Caunterburie*, in the time of RIC. the 1. did make their most abode at *Westminster*, as they do nowe at *Lambeth*, or *Lomehith*, and had ouer against the schoole that nowe is, a stately house : yet *Lelande* affirmeth the contrary, who saith, that the Bishops of *Caunterburie* haue continued at *Lambeth* since the *Normanes* comming into this land.

There is an auncient monument within the libertie of *Westminster*, called *Charing crosse*, erected about the yeere of Christ, 1290. by EDW.1. in memoriall of the death of *Elineor* his Queene, who died at *Hardlie* neere *Lincolne*, & was buried in *Westminster*.

The libertie of *Westminster* extendeth to *Temple bar*: so calcalled of the *Temple* within the same bar, and is called the bar for that it stoppeth and barreth the Mayor of *London*, as also the Magistrates of *Westminster*, that neither intrude vpon other. This bar or gate was throwne downe by the Kentish rebels, in the time of RIC.2.

Within

Parish Churches in the libertie of Westminster.

Within the libertie of *Westminster* are fower parish Churches, besides S. *Peters*, namelie,

S. *Margarets*

S. *Martynes* neere *Charing crosse*.

The *Sauoy* Church.

S. *Clements*, called Saint *Clements Dacorum*, or Saint *Clements Danes*.

The Sanctuary.

In the time of superstition there was in *Westminster*, a place called the *Sanctuary*, of an old Mosaical ryte, vsed among the *Israelites*, among whom euery tribe had certaine cities, and places of refuge, to which malefactors might repaire, and for a time be protected from the rigor of the law.

The Woollstaple.

There was at *Westminster* kept a staple of wooll, and is at this daie, called the *Woolstaple*, established in the time of EDWARD the 3.

The Sauoy.

The *Sauoye* was first built (as M. *Stowe* hath recorde) by *Peter* Earle of *Sauoy*, who was after made Earle of *Richmonde*, by HENRIE the 3. who called it the *Sauoy* after his Countrie. But

Pollid. Virg.

Poll. Virg. alloweth him not Earle of *Sauoy*, but calleth him *Petrus sebaudiensis: Peter* a *Sauoyan*, or of the countrie of *Sauoy*, who as the same *Poll.* affirmeth, buylt the same, and called it the *Sauoy*, of his natiue Countrey *Sauoye*. It was belonging vnto the Duke of *Lancaster*, in the time of R I C. the 2. in whose time it was wasted, burned, and spoyled by the Kentish rebels, about the yere 1381. It was reedefied by HEN. 7. by whose last will, it was intended to be finished, and made an Hospitall, for the reliefe of a 100. poore people, which was perfourmed by the most famous HEN. the 8. his sonne, and sufficiently furnished with lande, and reuenues, for the maintenance thereof.

Howses of Queene Elizabeths within Westminster.

Queene ELIZABETH hath within the precincts of this Citie three faire and pleasant pallaces: namely *White hall*, begun by Cardinall *Woolsey*, and finished, with manie most princely delights, by HEN. 8. S. *Ieames*, erected by the same king HEN. 8. and *Somerset* house builded by the Duke of *Somerset* about the yeere of Christ 1549.

Burgley *house*.

There are other houses worthy to be remembred within this libertie of *Westminster* as Burghley house, founded and erected by the right honorable S. *William Cycell* knight, Lord *Burghley*, Lord high treasoror of England.

Durham *house builded.*

Durham or *Dunelme* house sometime belonging to the Bishop of *Durham*, it was builded by one *Anthony Becke* in the time of RICHARD the third. Other famous houses of nobility are in this precinct, which to mention I omit for breuitie.

Places

Places diſtinguiſhed in the Map of
Weſtminſter by theſe letters and
figures following.

A. The Abbey.
B. Weſtminſter hall.
D. Long ditche.
E. Theuing lane.
F. The Amnerie.
G. The way to Toothill fielde.
H. The Lord *Dacres.*
I. Lord *Grayes.*
K. Kings ſtreete.
L. Round Woulſtaple.
M. The Parke lodgings.
N. The Tilt-yard.
O. S. Martynes in the field.
P. Clements Inne.
Q. New Inne.
R. S. Clements Danes.
S. Temple barre.
V. Drurie lane.
Y. The Gatehouſe.
2. S. Margarets.
3. S. Stephens alley.
5. Petite Fraunce.
6. H. 7. Chappell.
7. Deanes yarde.
8. Tennies Courtes.
9. Way to Hounſlow.
10. The Powder houſe.
11. White hall Orchard.
12. The Queenes Garden.
13. Staple Inne.

This Citie of *Weſtminſter* is knowne to haue no generall trade whereby releefe might be adminiſtred vnto the common ſort, as by Marchandize, clothing, or ſuch like, whereby the common wealth of a Citie is maineteined, and the inferiour people ſet to worke, had they not therefore ſome other meanes, the common ſort could nor be ſuſteined.

The firſt and principall meane whereby they are releeued, is hir Maieſties reſidence at *White hall*, or S. *Ieanes*, whence if hir grace

The chiefe meane whereby Weſtminſter is releeued.

grace be long abfent, the poore people forthwith complaine of penury and want, of a hard and miferable world. And therefore doe the people in manner generally feeme to power forth dayly petitions, that it might pleafe God to draw hir Maieftie to be refident at one of thefe places, whereat they reioyce and fare long the better. The like defire of hir Royall prefence haue other places, where hir Maiefties Pallaces are placed. And hir Maieftie in gracious confideration of their eftates, doth vifit them as it were *Alternis vicebus*, by turne at hir highnes pleafure, more for the comfort and releefe of the poore people, then for hir owne priuate delight. Therefore yee Citizens of *Weftminfter*, and other, whatfoeuer, forget not to be thankefull to the the Almightie for hir Royall prefence, hartely praying the King of Kings, to maintaine hir a profpering Queene long and many yeeres, and euery faithfull hart will ioyne with you, hauing alfo the benefite of hir bleffed inclination.

The fecond meane, the Tearmes. The feconde meane whereby this poore Citie is maintained, and the people releeued, is by the fower Termes in the yeere, for it hath pleafed God to eftablifh there, the place where Iuftice, lawe, and euerie mans right is (God graunt it) with equall ballance, indifferently adminiftred : whereunto great multitudes of people, vfually flocke, whofe refort although the Citie enioie but in the forenoone, yet yeeldeth their prefence, manie pence to the poore towne.

The hearing of caufes remooued to Yorke. There was in the time of E DW. 1. a difcontinuance of the lawe, in this Citie, and was thence remooued to *Yorke*, where it continued, feauen yeeres after reduced to the former place. It hath beene often difcontinued by the disfauour of Princes, and their conceiued difpleafure againft the inhabitants of the place, for difobedience, as a generall punifhment. Receiue this ye inhabitants of *Weftminfter*, as a neceffarie premonition, that ye reft carefull and vigilant, leaft the king of kings moouc her Maieftie to place the determination of caufes elfe where, which now is vnto you no fmall fupport.

The third mean, the Parliament. The third and laft meane (though it come feldome) is that great and generall convencion of all the eftates of this lande, the high Court of Parleament, which draweth vnto it a great acceffe of noble perfons, and others, to the place of affemblie, which is alfo fet moft gratioufly within this Citie, which yeeldeth no fmall releefe vnto the fame, which alfo(as is recorded in hiftories) hath beene holden at diuers other places in this land.

The tearme remoooued to Hertford. It is not yet forgotten, no doubt, how the God offended, vifited not onely this Citie, but alfo *London*, with a dangerous late infection, infomuch as the laft *Michaelmas* Terme was remoooued to

Hertford

Hertforde caſtle, which pinched the poore, and made the rich to complaine, in both theſe Cities: yet a more gentle forewarning of his diſpleaſure he cannot ſhew, who longing for new obedience in vs, calleth vs by diuers meanes, and without ſpeedie and harty repentance we ſhall likewiſe periſh.

The principal high waies from London
through *Middleſex*, and towards what eſpe-
ciall places in England they lead.

THe way noted with this figure 2. leadeth to Stanes, & thence towards Sariſburie, Exeter and other places in the weſt.

3. Leadeth to Colnebrooke, towardes Windſore, Reading, Bath, Briſtow, &c.

4. To Vxbridge, and ſo towardes Oxford, Glouceſter, & ſouth Wales.

5. To Egewoorth, towards Woodſtocke, Buckingham, Warwicke, Stafford, Worceſter, Cheſter, and north Wales.

6. To S. Albans, towards Bedford, Northampton, Leiceſter, Darby, &c.

7. Towardes Waltham, Hartforde, Bedforde, Huntingdon, Cambridge, into Norfolke: towardes Lincolne, Yorke and the Northen parts.

9. To Stratford on the Bow, and ſo into Eſſex and Suffolke.

10. Leadeth into Surrey and Suſſex.

11. To Kingſton vpon Thamis, Guyldford, Farneham, Wincheſter, Arrondell, Chechiſter, Southampton, Porteſmouth, &c.

Noble men, and Gentlemen, for the
moſt part, hauing houſes, or reſidence,
within this Shire.

A.

ſir *Ed. Anderſon*, Lord chiefe iuſtice of the common plees   pag. 21.

George Aſhbie.   16.

    Atee.   17.

    Alleley at *Daleſon* bill.   18.

B.

L. *Burghley*, L. high Treaſurer of England.   38.

    Barnes.   37.

William Burrowes at lymehouſe. 36.

Richard Bellamy.

The Buſhop of *London.* 20.

C.

L. *Compton.*   37. 41.

    Corbet.   21.

    Cornewell.   18.

    Cockeram at Hamſted. 22

Iohn Cunſtable at old Ford. 37.

    Cornewallies.   22.

    Carie at Maribone park.

D.

E. of *Darby* at Iſtleworth. 17.

H   L.

F I N I S.

I craue patience though I haue not giuen to euerie man his
addition of *Esquire* or *Gent.* for that I may easely erre therein,without the especiall aide of an expert Herault.

To the right worſhipful M. WILLIAM WAADE
Eſquire, one of the clearks of hir Maiesties
moſt Honorable priuie Counſell.

SIR, I cannot reſt vnreadie in deſire, to yeeld requitall
of your aide extended towards the publication of this
firſt part of my SPECVLVM BRITANNIAE: wherin
I muſt, and do thankfullie acknowledge your good inclination not towards me onely, but to all ſuch as indeuour matters tending to publike good. In lieu therfore of a farther faithful
recompence, accept, I beſeech you, my willing indeuor, vntil time
afforde ablenes to make better repay.

In magnis & voluiſſe dat eſt,
I. N.

A I Lettori.

HA ſpeſo molti dí per Amor voſtro.
A pinger queſte carte famigliare,
Citte, caſtelli, fiume deliniare,
Le terre miſurar Nordeno noſtro
Non guardate à le carte, ne à l'inchioſtro
Perche è vna coſa, che non ſa parlare
Guardate pur ſe l'opra vi può entrare
Se'l ſpecchio ui piace, che vi moſtro

Non otioſa, mà faticoſa impreſa
è queſto ſpecchio del Britanno lido.
Non è compoſto ſenza molta ſpeſa
Non cercano tal' opr' alcuno nido.
Norden il ſpecchio tuo ſenza conteſa
Riſplenderà doù è più chiaro il grido.

Ar. Oln.

Ingenuo lectori, de opere, & Au-
thore tetraſtichon.

QVem tulit is punctum, qui miſcuit vtile dulci;
Nordenus tulit hunc, vtile, dulce canens.
Vtile, dulce canit, digni laude ille, liberque:
Nam placet, & prodeſt, vtile, dulce, canens.

Notitia nobile nomen:
Robertus Nicolſonus.

Sur le Miroir de grand Bretaigne, de *M. Iehan Norden.*

GArdez, gentils, regardez cest' ouurage,
  Tres-doctes Dames, & tres-sages, Sieurs :
  Moult delectant voz yeulx, voz sens, & coeurs,
Cy fait Plaisir, auec Profit mariage.

Chacun Degre, rumine, chachun Aage,
  Ce petit liure, plein de grands doulceurs :
  Rend luy louange, qui doulces rend odeurs,
Que chacun fait, qui est sçauant ou sage.

Les autres sont autheurs d' Enui', & vice,
  Ennemis a vertu, sciens, & Notice,
  Vilipendans les œuures de sçauoir :

Mais nobles, doctes, & gentils esprits,
  Qui compte tiennent des elegans escripts,
  Hault priseront N O R D E N son cler Miroir.

N' ayant espour qu' en Dieu.
Robert Nicolson.

Corrections.

† In pag. 11. line 5. for *eighteene*, read *thirteene*.
‡ In pag. 21. for *Io. Fortescue* esquire, read sir *Iohn Fortescue* knight.
‡ In pag 27. for 5191. read 3911.
  In the same pag. for *Antonius*, read *Antoninus.*
  In pag. 47. for *Staple Inne*, read *Lyons Inne.*